Walter Butler Cheadle

**The Various Manifestations of the Rheumatic State as exemplified in Childhood and Early Life**

Walter Butler Cheadle

**The Various Manifestations of the Rheumatic State as exemplified in Childhood and Early Life**

ISBN/EAN: 9783337372361

Printed in Europe, USA, Canada, Australia, Japan

Cover: Foto ©ninafisch / pixelio.de

More available books at **www.hansebooks.com**

# THE VARIOUS MANIFESTATIONS

OF THE

# RHEUMATIC STATE

AS EXEMPLIFIED IN

CHILDHOOD AND EARLY LIFE

LECTURES DELIVERED BEFORE

THE HARVEIAN SOCIETY OF LONDON

BY

W. B. CHEADLE, M.D.

PHYSICIAN TO ST MARY'S HOSPITAL, AND LECTURER ON MEDICINE ST MARY'S
MEDICAL SCHOOL; SENIOR PHYSICIAN TO THE HOSPITAL FOR
SICK CHILDREN, GREAT ORMOND STREET

LONDON
SMITH, ELDER, & CO., 15 WATERLOO PLACE
1889

# PREFACE

THESE LECTURES were originally published in the *Lancet*; and I have to express my thanks to the proprietors of that journal for their courtesy in permitting their early reproduction in the present form.

W. B. C.

19 PORTMAN STREET, W.
    *June* 15, 1889.

## LECTURE III.

Pericarditis—Its connection with other phases of rheumatism—Special characteristics in childhood—Subacute, recurrent, dry—Tendency to fibrosis and chronic thickening rather than to effusion—Endocarditis; subacute and recurrent likewise—Special liability of children and of young girls—Connection of endocarditis with other phases of rheumatism—The endocarditis of chorea—Relation of pericarditis and endocarditis to the evolution of nodules—Morbid changes in nodules and cardiac valves analogous—Significance of this—Different forms of valvular disease—Mitral stenosis—Early signs—Double second sound at the apex—Hypertrophy and dilatation—Comparative rarity of dropsy—The mode of death differs from that met with in adults—Scarlatinal rheumatism—Rheumatoid arthritis—Special points in treatment . . . . . . . . . . . . 79

# THE VARIOUS MANIFESTATIONS OF THE
# RHEUMATIC STATE

AS EXEMPLIFIED IN

# CHILDHOOD AND EARLY LIFE

BEING THE HARVEIAN LECTURES FOR 1888.

## LECTURE I.

Rheumatism not to be regarded as a mere affection of the joints—Arthritis only one of many rheumatic phenomena—Various phases of the rheumatic state—General characteristics of the rheumatism of childhood as compared with that of adults—Comparative insignificance of the joint affection—Greater prominence and frequency of other phases—Tendency of the various phenomena of the rheumatic series to appear independently—They may occur singly, or in various combinations, in varying order of sequence, at different intervals of time—Examples—Influence of sex—Influence of inherited tendency—The rheumatic phenomena considered in detail—Arthritis—Special characters in childhood—Variation in the chief symptoms from the adult type.

THERE is perhaps no serious disease more familiar to us than acute articular rheumatism; it is one of the disorders most commonly seen in the wards of a general hospital; it is constantly encountered in private practice; and I must confess that when I chose Rheumatism as the subject of the Lectures which you have done me the honour to ask me to deliver, I was almost afraid that it might be deemed too trite and commonplace, destitute of sufficient novelty and interest. But there is a certain advantage in treating of a matter with which the audience are familiar, and I trust I shall be able to present it to you in some new aspects, and to attract attention to certain points of great interest, hitherto, I think, insufficiently considered; and thus I hope that my choice may be justified, and any unfavourable criticism in this respect eventually disarmed.

I must premise, at the outset, that in these Lectures I shall use the terms 'rheumatism' and 'rheumatic' in the strictest sense, as applying only to that form which is distinguished as acute or genuine rheumatism, of which what is known as rheumatic fever is the most extreme expression in adults, but which appears with every degree of acuteness and severity, and also, as I hope to show, in many different phases.

Acute articular rheumatism is not only an extremely common disease, but it has very striking and obvious symptoms by which it is readily recognised; the swollen, tender, painful joints, the fever, the profuse sour-smelling perspirations, render a typical case unmistakable and distinct; yet this is a picture of the disease very rarely seen in childhood. Even in its milder forms, genuine articular rheumatism preserves its special features; some may be absent, others modified; yet the stiffness, tenderness, and swelling of joints usually indicate the nature of the affection. But this, again, does not represent rheumatism completely as seen in childhood. We are so accustomed to associate the term 'rheumatism' with this condition of the joints, to regard arthritis as the chief and essential feature, and any associated affections of other parts as mere complications, that it is difficult at first to realise that articular inflammation is only one of many direct and sometimes independent manifestations of the rheumatic state. This is, however, the one central idea which I wish to enforce. The ordinary conception of acute rheumatism, as essentially characterised by articular inflammation, is based upon observation of the disease as we see it in adults; in them the arthritis is one of the most constant, prominent, and characteristic of the morbid phenomena which arise. The names rheumarthritis, polyarthritis, polyarthritis synovialis, and polyarthritis rheumatica acuta, reflect this narrow view.

A study of the disease in children, however, leads to a far wider conception. In the rheumatism of early life other morbid conditions appear prominently and constantly, which may claim, equally with the arthritis, to be regarded as direct results of rheumatic activity; in childhood arthritis cannot be regarded as alone typical, essential, and representative.

The most complete and comprehensive manifestation of the various phases of rheumatism belongs, indeed, to the period of childhood; it appears then, under the simplest condition; this presentation of the disease should be regarded as representative, and the changes which take place in the phenomena with advancing age regarded as modifications of the earlier and more perfect form. I will ask you, gentlemen, to put aside, at any rate for the moment, this limited and narrow view of rheumatism as inseparably associated with arthritis, a view based upon observation of the disease in grown persons, and to look at it from a new standpoint.

There are certain affections which have been observed to be so frequently associated with acute rheumatism that the existence of some pathological connection between them has come to be very generally accepted, although the extent and intimacy of the association may be a matter of controversy.

Endocarditis and pericarditis, for example, are so constantly seen as immediate accompaniments of articular rheumatism, even in adults, that there is no question of their relation to it; and in the case of children the connection is still more frequent and more intimate. Pleurisy, again, and tonsillitis are allowed to be not unfrequently accompaniments of articular rheumatism in both periods of life. But with these I think the list ends as far as adults are concerned. If we turn to children, however, we learn that the scope of acute rheumatism is wider still. Other manifestations appear in undoubted association with it in early life, and must be included in the series of rheumatic phases, although some decline or disappear in later life. Subcutaneous tendinous nodules, chorea, and exudative erythema are (the first I think always, the two latter commonly) developments of rheumatism. There are other affections which have been deemed by some to be minor expressions of the rheumatic diathesis. I have not satisfied myself upon this point, and I wish to limit the list to those generally accepted as having some connection with it. The claims of endocarditis, of pericarditis, of pleurisy, of tonsillitis, of exudative erythema, of chorea, of subcutaneous nodules, will hardly, I think, be seriously disputed. I shall have something to say on this point when I come to speak of them in detail; but for my present purpose I shall assume the connection and speak of these seven phases, together with arthritis, as the rheumatic series.

Let me not be misunderstood in this matter however. I do not say that the rheumatic poison, or whatever the morbid influence may be, is the sóle cause of these affections associated with rheumatic arthritis, any more than it is the sole cause of inflammation of joint structures. They are set up by other causes, just as arthritis, for example, may be set up by mechanical injury, by the poison of gout, or that of septicæmia or pyæmia. Yet the rheumatic poison is the most common exciting cause of arthritis, and so with other members of the rheumatic series. Take, for instance, pericarditis, endocarditis, and pleurisy. The most common cause of the first two, at any rate, is rheumatism. Yet these same inflammations of the pericardium, endocardium, and pleura are now and again set up by the septic or pyæmic poison, or that of uræmia. Tonsillitis, erythema, and chorea in like manner are undoubtedly set up by other exciting causes as well as by rheumatism, although the latter is a frequent and potent one. The only manifestation of the series absolutely and solely rheumatic, never stirred up, as far as I know, by any stimulus except the rheumatic stimulus, is the evolution of subcutaneous tendinous nodules.

It appears, then, that the rheumatic virus (whatever its exact nature and by whatever physiological machinery it acts) which produces the articular inflammation produces in like manner inflammation of the fibrous tissue of the pericardium, endocardium, and pleura, and that of fasciæ and tendons. It has clearly an irritant inflammatory effect upon fibrous tissue, not of the joints alone but of these other structures. It affects, moreover, mucous membrane and skin, and disturbs nervous centres. The conception of rheumatism, then, which I shall endeavour to put forward and establish is this broad one; that the terms 'rheumatism' and 'rheumatic' must be held to include many various morbid expressions—the series of phenomena I have laid down—and must not be regarded as a special inflammation of tendons and ligaments or synovial membranes, or as a condition of which this is always the chief feature, accompanied by complications and sequelæ. The term 'diathesis' is quite inadequate; there is something more than mere tendency—a common factor concerned in the production of those different phases—and forming the link between.

The rheumatism of childhood exhibits a marked

contrast to the disease as it is seen in mature life. The articular affection, which is regarded as the very type and essence of the latter, has not yet become the chief feature, but is usually slight and subordinate, and, indeed, may be absent altogether from a seizure undoubtedly rheumatic in its nature; while other phases, again, less marked in the disease of adult life, or even absent from it altogether, rule as prominent and characteristic features. The joint tissues are less susceptible; the other fibrous tissues more so. Subcutaneous nodules, which are so frequent and significant in early life, practically disappear with the advent of puberty; and chorea, so common in connection with the rheumatism of childhood, disappears as full maturity is reached. Endocarditis and pericarditis, again, frequent as they are in adult life, are more frequent still in children—i.e. they tend to decline as age advances.[1] In the rheumatism of early life arthritis is at its minimum; endocarditis, pericarditis, chorea, and subcutaneous nodules at their maximum. As life advances this is gradually reversed; the joint

[1] The statistics of the Collective Investigation Committee of the British Medical Association (*British Medical Journal*, Feb. 1888) give 72 per cent. of heart-disease in rheumatism in the case of children, as compared with 46 per cent. in male adults. In the case of female adults the difference is not so marked—i.e. they retain in some degree the special proclivity of childhood.

affection becomes more prominent, constant, and typical of the disease, and reaches its maximum; while the other phenomena decline and tend to die out. So that, if the picture of the disease had been drawn originally (as it should be) from the rheumatism of childhood, the articular affection would not have been taken as representative, or endocarditis and pericarditis spoken of as complications. Endocarditis or chorea would have been taken as the primary essential phenomena, and the articular affection as a complication. Yet none are really to be regarded as complications. When, for instance, any of these phases—pericarditis, nodules, or chorea—occur in immediate association with arthritis, they are in no way set up by the arthritis; they may come before it or after it, or occur quite independently. And so with the articular affection: the various phases are not complications or sequelæ, but direct manifestations of rheumatic activity.

Another point of distinction between the rheumatism of childhood and that of later life is the tendency of the various phases to arise independently and apart from each other. They do, indeed, occur grouped together commonly enough, as in adult life; but often also the series of rheumatic events is spread out, scattered over a period of months or years, so that the history of a rheumatism may be the history of childhood. There may be, for instance, an endocarditis at one time, a chorea at another, a tonsillitis at another, without any other manifestation at the moment, and yet each may be as essentially an expression of rheumatism as the articular affection which may perhaps have happened long before or does not appear until long after. Look, for instance, at Series VIII., in the abstracts of cases in the table, showing the succession of rheumatic events—the first event was chorea, the articular affection not occurring until eleven months later; or at Series II., where the first event was an endocarditis which had occurred years at least before any arthritis was observed; or at Series X., where there were two attacks of chorea before the arthritis appeared. There was nothing, under the present system of taking articular affection as the key to the condition, to show that the chorea or endocarditis were rheumatic at the time they occurred. More usually, however, two or three phases occur more or less closely together; as, for instance, the common coincidence of arthritis with endocarditis (as in Series I.), or chorea, nodules, and endocarditis.

The rheumatic series as seen in children may, indeed, be complete or incomplete in any degree. The whole series may follow in succession or it may be limited to a single event—even an arthritis only, or a chorea only, or an endocarditis only, without subsequent development of any other rheumatic seizure. Again, the combinations of the different phases of the rheumatic series may follow any order of sequence. Sometimes—most commonly—an arthritis first; sometimes a chorea first, or an endocarditis. We are so accustomed to regard arthritis as the starting-point, and other manifestations as complications or sequelæ, that the possibly rheumatic nature of the affections which come before it is liable to be overlooked. Yet these manifestations, developed previously to arthritis, cannot be looked upon as complications or sequelæ, for there is no arthritis to complicate or follow. They are direct and independent results of the rheumatic disturbance. Further, these phases of the rheumatic series may be either closely associated in point of time, singly or in groups, or scattered, with varying intervals between. Here, again, we are so accustomed to look at the short series of adult rheumatism, minus chorea and nodules, occurring in conjunction with arthritis, that even a group of significant affections occurring apart from arthritis would hardly be recognised as rheumatic. And so on with the other members of the morbid series, some of which, again, may be repeated more than once. Clinical examples, from cases actually observed, will serve to illustrate most clearly some of the various combinations and the wide range and protean character of rheumatism in children. The most frequent of all is the one with which we are so familiar in adults.

*Series I.*—(1) Arthritis; (2) endocarditis; these may recur more than once without other phases. H. B. K——, a boy of nine, was brought to the Hospital for Sick Children in January 1888, with rheumatism of the joints and advanced mitral disease. Here the arthritis recurred almost yearly, and probably the endocarditis also, for when examined in 1888 there were marked thrill, a double murmur at the apex, and enormous hypertrophy and dilatation; while the chorea did not appear until six years after the first arthritis. Often in childhood to these two manifestations are added the development of nodules, and perhaps pericarditis or pleurisy.

*Series II.*—C. H. B—— was brought to the Hospital for Sick Children in May, 1888, for pains in the knees and in various joints. Small subcutaneous nodules were found on the knees, elbows, and malleoli. He had had pains in the back of the knees and in the ankles for the previous five weeks, never before. There was a double mitral murmur with great hypertrophy. Pleurisy developed on June 7th; then a fresh crop of nodules on June 9th; pericarditis on June 11th, and again on July 14th; a fresh crop of nodules on July 14th. With this came excited action of the heart; the pulse rose to 140, marking the advent of fresh endocarditis and probably of pericarditis. Pleurisy (slight) followed on August 16th; after this, gradual failure, and death on September 6th. In this case the primary endocarditis must have occurred some years before the pains in the joints were first noted, which was only five weeks before admission, whereas the heart-disease was of long standing, as evidenced by the great hypertrophy. It is to be noted, too, in this case how endocarditis, pericarditis, and pleurisy coincided with the appearance of fresh crops of nodules.

Another common combination is that represented in

*Series III.*—(1) Arthritis and endocarditis; (2) chorea. George S——, aged seven years and a-half, was admitted for right parétic hemichorea. He had had rheumatic arthritis seven months before, accompanied by endocarditis, evidenced by a loud mitral murmur. Two months later he had chorea; then a second attack, for which he was admitted. There was a family history of rheumatism; the father had had rheumatic fever; the mother chorea as a child.

## CLINICAL EXAMPLES OF DIFFERENT COMBINATIONS

| Series I. | Series II. | Series III. | Series IV. | Series V. |
|---|---|---|---|---|
| H. B. K., boy aged nine. (Hosp. Sick Children, 1888.) | C. H. B., boy aged five. (Hosp. Sick Children, 1888.) | G. S., aged seven. (Hospital Sick Children.) | H. C., aged ten. (Hospital Sick Children, 1878.) | A. W., aged sixteen. (St. Mary's Hosp.) |
| 1. { Arthritis, Endocarditis. (1882.) | 1. Endocarditis (?) | 1. { Arthritis, Endocarditis. | 1. { Chorea, Endocarditis (1875.) | 1. { Chorea, Endocarditis. (1874.) |
| 2. { Arthritis, Endocarditis. (1884.) | 2. { Arthritis, evolution of Nodules. (March, 1888.) | 2. { Chorea five months later. | 2. { Mitral Disease found. (1878.) | 2. { Mitral disease found with— Arthritis four years later (1878.) |
| 3. { Arthritis, Endocarditis (1885. Recurring almost yearly for 6 years.) | 3. { Second crop of Nodules, Pleurisy, Pericarditis. (June, 1888.) | 3. { Chorea after two months' interval. (Father had rheumatic fever; mother had chorea as a child.) | 3. { Arthritis absent. (Mother rheumatic fever and heart disease.) | — |
| 4. { Arthritis, Endocarditis. (1886.) | 4. { Third crop of Nodules, fresh Endocarditis, fresh Pericarditis. (July, 1888.) | — | — | — |
| 5. { Arthritis, Endocarditis. (1887.) | 5. { Pleurisy, Pericarditis (recurrent). (August, 1888.) | — | — | — |
| 6. { Arthritis, Chorea. (1888.) | — | — | — | — |

OF VARIOUS PHASES OF THE RHEUMATIC SERIES.

| | Series VI. | | Series VII. | | Series VIII. | | Series IX. | | Series X. |
|---|---|---|---|---|---|---|---|---|---|
| | A.B., aged twelve. (St. Mary's Hosp., 1884.) | | F. M. C., aged seven. | | W. S., aged four years and a-half. (Hosp. Sick Ch., 1887.) | | F. M., aged five (Hosp. Sick Ch., 1888.) | | John T., aged seven. (Hosp. Sick Children, Dec. 1887.) |
| 1. | ARTHRITIS, ENDOCARDITIS. (1881.) | 1. | ARTHRITIS (severe), TONSILLITIS. (1878.) | 1. | CHOREA probably accompanied by ENDOCARDITIS. (Nov. 1886.) | 1. | ARTHRITIS. (Sept. 1887.) | 1. | CHOREA, attributed to fright. (Nov. 1886.) |
| 2. | CHOREA. (Dec. 1884.) Old-standing MITRAL DISEASE discovered. | 2. | PURPURA RHEUMATICA. (1883.) | 2. | Interval of eleven months. ARTHRITIS, first attack. (Oct. 1887.) | 2. | ARTHRITIS (second attack.) (Jan. 1888.) | 2. | CHOREA (second attack), likewise attributed to fright. (Aug. 1887.) |
| 3. | PERICARDITIS. (Jan. 1885.) | 3. | CHOREA (1883.) | 3. | CHOREA (second attack), SUBCUTANEOUS NODULES, ENDOCARDITIS, ERYTHEMA MARGINATUM (Nov. 1887.) | 3. | CHOREA, eruption of NODULES, ENDOCARDITIS (first attack). (March, 1888.) ARTHRITIS (third attack). (April.) ERYTHEMA MARGINATUM. | 3. | ARTHRITIS, evolution of NODULES. (Nov. 1887.) ENDOCARDITIS. (Dec.) |
| | — | 4. | TONSILLITIS, constantly recurring for several years. (1883–4–5.) | 4. | EMOTIONAL ATTACKS, CHOREA (continued), FRESH NODULES. (Dec. 1887.) | 4. | CHOREA (second attack), eruption of NODULES (second attack.) (Dec. 1888.) | 4. | CHOREA (third attack), EMOTIONAL ATTACKS, LARGE NODULES (second eruption), ARTHRITIS (second attack), ENDOCARDITIS, PERICARDITIS, PLEURISY. (June, 1888.) |
| | — | | — | 5. | ERYTHEMA MARGINATUM, fresh eruption of NODULES, CHOREA (relapse), ARTHRITIS (second attack). (Jan. 1888.) | | — | 5. | ENDOCARDITIS, PERICARDITIS. (July, 1888.) DEATH, Aug. 1888. |
| | — | | — | 6. | Fresh eruption of ERYTHEMA, fresh crop of NODULES, TONSILLITIS. (Feb. 1888.) DEATH, March 1888. | | — | | — |

Sometimes the arthritis appears to be missing. Thus:—

*Series IV.*—Henry C——, aged ten years and a-half, was admitted to Great Ormond Street, June 1878, with mitral stenosis and regurgitation and great hypertrophy. He had never had any joint affection, but he had had chorea three years before. It was found, moreover, that his mother had had rheumatic fever, and was suffering from valvular disease of the heart resulting from it. I think that in this case the morbus cordis must be reasonably attributed to rheumatic endocarditis; the chorea to rheumatic influence likewise, although no arthritis had appeared up to the time of observation.

The combination in which the articular affection appears last in the series throws much light on such cases as the preceding. Here is an example:—

*Series V.*—Alice W——, aged sixteen, admitted into St. Mary's Hospital complaining of pain, stiffness, and tenderness of knees and ankles. On examining the chest, well-marked mitral disease of old standing was found—viz. a loud regurgitant murmur, with great hypertrophy and dilatation. The original endocarditis must have taken place years before. Yet, observe, she was not known to have had any joint affection before the present attack; but she had had chorea four years before, and, moreover, her mother had had rheumatic fever; her mother's sister had had rheumatic fever. Can there be any reasonable doubt that both chorea and endocarditis (which, no doubt, occurred with the chorea four years before the articular rheumatism) were both of them rheumatic? Yet, until the articular affection appeared, which was delayed to the age of sixteen, this case was exactly similar to the preceding. If the chorea and accompanying endocarditis had been recorded at the time of their occurrence, there would have been nothing to stamp them as rheumatic, and the endocarditis would have been styled 'choreic.' The appearance of acute articular rheumatism afterwards, and the family history of the disease in mother and aunt, revealed the link between the different phases.

Another combination, where arthritis and endocarditis commence the series and pericarditis and chorea follow later on, is thus shown:—

*Series VI.*—A. B——, a girl of twelve, was admitted into St. Mary's Hospital in 1884 for severe chorea. She had had rheumatic fever three years before; she had also had endocarditis, as evidenced by a loud mitral murmur. The chorea rapidly got well under arsenic; but just at this point acute pericarditis came on. There was not the slightest affection of the joints, yet I take it both chorea and pericarditis were rheumatic.

You will observe that either endocarditis or pericarditis is present in each of the preceding series. Yet these most serious of all the rheumatic phases, present, as I have said, in nearly three-fourths of articular affections in children, are sometimes wanting. Happily this was so in the case of one of my own boys, and his history also illustrates the connection of two of the less prominent phenomena of the rheumatic series—viz. purpura rheumatica and tonsillitis.

*Series VII.*—F. M. C——, a boy of seven, had acute articular rheumatism, with tonsillitis, in 1878. There was no endocarditis or pericarditis or other manifestation—arthritis and tonsillitis only; and for several years there was complete quiescence of rheumatic activity. Then in 1883, or five years after the arthritis, purpura rheumatica appeared; this was unaccompanied by any other phase. Then, about one year later, chorea and emotional attacks occurred. Finally, he had tonsillitis, recurring frequently and severely for four or five years.

In all the examples yet given the rheumatic series has been incomplete, as indeed it is most commonly, many of the minor phases especially being wanting.

This is, however, partly due no doubt to the imperfection of the record, many of the cases being taken before the significance of subcutaneous nodules, tonsillitis, and erythema was fully recognised.

I will add, therefore, in conclusion of this part of the subject, three more combinations, in which the series is fuller and almost complete.

*Series VIII.*—Look at the remarkable succession of rheumatic events, occurring chiefly in groups, given in this series. W. S——, a boy of five, was recently under my care in the Children's Hospital. The first event was an attack of chorea in November, 1886, when the boy was between three and four years old. This was almost certainly accompanied by endocarditis, for a double mitral disease of old standing was discovered on his admission to hospital a year later. The second event was an attack of articular rheumatism (the first), in October, 1887. The third group of events was a second attack of chorea, accompanied by an extraordinary development of subcutaneous nodules, and also by fresh endocarditis and erythema marginatum, in November, 1887. The fourth group of events was a series of emotional attacks, accompanied by further evolution of subcutaneous nodules and continued chorea, in December, 1887. The fifth group of events comprised a second eruption of erythema, a second eruption of subcutaneous nodules, a relapse of chorea, and (last in order) a second attack of arthritis, in January, 1888. The sixth group of events consisted of a third eruption of nodules, a third eruption of erythema, and tonsillitis, in February, 1888, followed by death in March. Here I would ask you to observe that the very first event of the series was chorea (probably accompanied by endocarditis), the first appearance of rheumatism of the joints being delayed until one year later; so that, if we take the joint affection as the test, there was nothing, when the chorea first occurred, to indicate its rheumatic nature; and it would no doubt have been classed as non-rheumatic, and the accompanying endocarditis simply termed 'choreic.' The rheumatic relation was only established by subsequent events, and the last phase was tonsillitis, in an unusual place, late in the series.

*Series IX.*—The next example (F. M——, aged five, Hospital for Sick Children, 1886) is not quite so complete, but represents a common sequence of events. The first was articular rheumatism in September, 1887. There was no other manifestation at the time. The next event was a second attack of articular rheumatism four months later (January, 1888); and this, again, was unaccompanied by any other manifestation. The third event came three months later still, when chorea developed, and this was accompanied by an eruption of large subcutaneous nodules, and with these the first sign of endocarditis, and also another phase—erythema marginatum. The fourth event, a month later still, consisted in a fresh eruption of nodules only, followed by convalescence and quiescence until December, 1888, when the boy was readmitted to hospital with a fifth rheumatic development, consisting of chorea and another eruption of nodules. This case presents the unusual feature of two attacks of arthritis without appreciable endocarditis. A soft murmur was first found, without hypertrophy, in the third period, together with the chorea, an evolution of nodules, and a slight arthritis of one wrist only.

*Series X.*—The last example which I have to give exhibits the rheumatic events in different order. J. T——, a boy of seven, was admitted to the Children's Hospital in December, 1887. The first event in his case was chorea, accompanied at the time by no other phase of rheumatism, and attributed to fright (November, 1886). The second event was a second attack, likewise unaccompanied by any other manifestation of rheumatism, and attributed to fright (August, 1887). Up to this period there had been no arthritis, but two months later it came in a group of phases comprising the third manifestation—viz. arthritis, evolution of large nodules, endocarditis (November and December, 1887); then a period of rest for nearly six months; after which came the fourth group of events, comprising a third attack of chorea with emotional seizures, a second eruption of nodules, pleurisy, pericarditis (June, 1888); and, lastly, the fifth and final manifestation—recurrent endocarditis, pericarditis (in July, 1888), and death (August, 1888), when the pericardium was found enormously thickened, the aortic and tricuspid valves thickened, and the mitral thickened to a remarkable degree. In this case, intensely rheumatic, which ended fatally, it is deserving of notice that two attacks of chorea at intervals of a year, both attributed to fright, preceded the first known attack of articular rheumatism; and also that the persistent endocarditis and pericarditis marched *pari passu* with the evolution of nodules.

Such, gentlemen, are some of the combinations of the rheumatic series. They are all taken from actual cases; but the list is not exhausted; the varieties are numerous, as numerous perhaps as the combinations and permutations possible with the eight phases I have named as commonly rheumatic.

But the brief summaries I have given will serve perhaps to exhibit the disease in its different outbreaks, extending over months or years, as one connected whole, instead of the fragmentary view afforded by a single phase, or the less numerous phenomena of the rheumatism of adult life.

Before I pass on to the consideration of each phase of rheumatism in detail there are two other characteristics of rheumatism in childhood to which I must make some allusion. One is the incidence of the disease upon the two sexes: the other the influence of inherited constitutional predisposition.

Taking first the influence of sex. The incidence of articular rheumatism upon males and females exhibits marked contrasts and variations at different periods of life. I ask your attention to this, because it has an important bearing upon the rheumatic connection of chorea and heart disease, which I shall have to point out later. Taking males and females of all ages together, articular rheumatism is somewhat more common in the former. The statistics of the Collective Investigation Committee of the British Medical Association [1] yield in 655 cases 375 males to 279 females.[2] Up to the age of twenty, however, the

[1] *Collective Investigation Record*, vol. iv. 1888, p. 67.

[2] The statistics collected by Senator from various sources (Ziemssen's *Cyclopædia*, vol. xvi. p. 18) give somewhat conflicting results;

balance is the other way. For this period there is a preponderance of females. The Collective Investigation Statistics yield 108 males to 120 females.[1] After twenty the males are enormously in excess— viz. 263 to 158.[2] Yet further, this preponderance of females over males in early life is not uniform at all periods of this first twenty years, but shows a remarkable variation, which is, I think, of considerable significance. Taking periods of five years from one to twenty years, it appears that in the first, one to five years of age, boys preponderate—viz. 5 to 1. At the next quinquennial period, between five and ten years, they become nearly equal—viz. 15 boys to 14 girls. At the next period, eleven to fifteen years of age inclusive, comes a remarkable change. The proportion is suddenly and decisively reversed. During this quinquennial period girls suffer from articular rheumatism in great preponderance—viz. 47

but collectively yield a similar preponderance of males—viz. 1499 to 1425 females.

[1] *Collective Investigation Record*, vol. iv. p. 67.

[2] The general preponderance of girls over boys is borne out by other statistics. The records of cases of articular rheumatism at the Children's Hospital in Great Ormond Street for twenty-six years give 336 girls to 327 boys. In this case the limit of age is for one period ten years, and for another twelve, so that it excludes a large proportion of cases between eleven and fifteen, when girls most predominate. Dr. Goodhart's statistics give 42 girls to 27 boys (Diseases of Children, p. 510).

girls to 25 boys, or nearly two to one. After fifteen there is another change; the greater liability of girls gradually declines up to twenty, so that at the close of this period males again preponderate—viz. 76 to 67.[1] The greater proclivity of females, which has been noted up to twenty years of age, is then, in reality, chiefly due to their extraordinary liability to the disease during this particular period of from eleven to fifteen. A strong confirmation of this special susceptibility of young girls to rheumatic arthritis is afforded by the fact that the rule holds with regard to scarlatinal rheumatism. According to the statistics of 652 cases of scarlatina at the South-Western Fever Hospital noted by Dr. Gresswell, to whom I am greatly indebted for calling my attention to the point and for this information, it appears that the incidence of scarlatinal arthritis in girls and boys between three and ten years of age is about equal, just as in ordinary rheumatic arthritis—viz. four boys in 176 cases, 5 girls in 179 cases; between ten and fifteen, boys 0 in 42, girls 4 in 71, again in harmony with the results in ordinary rheumatism. The numbers are small, but as far as they go support the special susceptibility of girls to rheumatic

[1] *Collective Investigation Record*, vol. iv. 1888. (Analysis of cases there given.)

arthritis.[1] So that, if these statistics hold good, girls from the age of ten to fifteen are about twice as liable to articular rheumatism as boys, in striking contrast to all other periods, when males preponderate. It will appear later that this greater liability of girls to rheumatic arthritis during this period corresponds with a similar liability to endocarditis and chorea.

The second point, the influence of family predisposition, comes out very clearly in the case of children. The tendency to rheumatism is transmitted as strongly as the tendency to gout. This is more striking than in the case of adults: partly, perhaps, for the reason that the constitutional tendency existing is usually excited into activity before maturity—if it is there, it comes out in childhood; and partly, perhaps, because of the greater ease with which the history of relatives is obtained in the case of children. The parents supply information about their own generation and that of their children; while grown persons, amongst the poor at any rate, know little, and forget much of the generation which

[1] The susceptibility appears, however, to be more prolonged than in simple rheumatism. Taking the period ten to twenty-five years, the numbers are: boys, 2 cases of arthritis out of 80 cases of scarlatina; girls, 12 cases out of 118. Yet this is, of course, on the whole, a further confirmation of the special liability of young females.

preceded them. The estimates of the extent of this transmission vary according to the minuteness of inquiry made, and the evidence allowed as sufficient to establish the existence of the rheumatic state. Sir A. Garrod traced it in about 25 per cent. Dr. A. B. Garrod,[1] taking adults and children together, estimates it at 35 per cent. in rheumatic patients, as compared with 20 per cent. in non-rheumatic patients. These estimates are necessarily under the mark, since they are founded solely upon the occurrence of well-marked attacks of acute articular rheumatism, and chiefly in adults, all evidence afforded by minor attacks or combination of other phases, such as heart disease, chorea, nodules, &c., not being taken into account. Dr. Goodhart,[2] taking children alone, found satisfactory evidence of rheumatic affection in 41 out of 69, or 57 per cent. The influence of hereditary predisposition is well shown by some statistics I have had drawn up, for which I am indebted to the late registrar at the Hospital for Sick Children, Dr. Chaffey. Taking 592 cases of children admitted for diseases of all kinds, both medical and surgical, careful inquiry was made into the family history with regard to acute rheumatism. In 173 there was clear history

---

[1] The *Lancet*, July 21, 1888.
[2] *Diseases of Children*, p. 512.

of acute rheumatism in immediate blood-relatives. Of these 173, 38 had developed unmistakable rheumatic affection, equal to 20 per cent. If slighter arthritis, chorea, heart disease, and other less certain manifestations, were admitted as evidence, this proportion would of course be largely increased. Taking now the remaining 319 in whom no history of joint affection in immediate blood-relatives could be traced, only 15 developed articular rheumatism, equal to 4·5 per cent. So that with a family history of acute rheumatism in immediate blood-relatives the chance of an individual with such hereditary tendency contracting acute articular rheumatism is nearly five times as great as that of an individual who has no such hereditary taint. I may give a few examples to illustrate this influence of family predisposition.

George L——, aged eight, was admitted to Great Ormond Street for advanced mitral disease of the heart. He had had rheumatic fever four years before, followed by two attacks of chorea. His father had rheumatic fever as a child, and died of valvular disease of the heart. His father's sister had rheumatic fever three times. The father's brother had subacute rheumatism.

Take another instance. George H. S——, aged nine years and five months, was admitted to Great

Ormond Street with slight articular rheumatism, ushered in by tonsillitis. On examination a loud mitral regurgitant murmur and an aortic regurgitant murmur were found, with great hypertrophy. He must have had endocarditis long before, yet there was no history of any previous joint affection. His mother had had rheumatic fever; his mother's sister rheumatic fever, followed by chorea; another sister of the mother rheumatic fever; the father had rheumatism, but of doubtful nature.

But these instances of family predisposition, of which I could furnish almost any number, are quite eclipsed by a case published by Dr. Goodhart in vol. xxv. of Guy's Hospital Reports, where, 'with a rheumatic strain in both father and mother, five out of six children under fifteen—i.e. all but a baby of fourteen months—had either articular rheumatism or heart-disease. A boy of fifteen had had rheumatic fever twice, and had mitral regurgitation; the second, a boy of ten, the same; the third, a girl of eight, died of mitral disease; the fourth, a girl, had rheumatic fever after scarlatina, followed by mitral disease; the fifth, a boy of four, was laid by all winter with rheumatism.' And Dr. Goodhart mentions the case recorded by Steiner in his 'Diseases of Children,' which shows this proclivity in a still more extraordinary degree. A rheumatic mother had twelve children, and eleven of them had rheumatism before the age of twenty. Now it occurred to me that this extraordinary tendency of rheumatism to develop in certain families might be due to some special faults of locality or circumstances, but careful inquiry into a number of cases showed me that they arose in very various localities, in members of the family when in different places and under different conditions.

Having thus reviewed broadly the general characteristics of the rheumatism of childhood—viz. the comparative insignificance of the articular affection; the prominence and importance of other phenomena, some of which, such as nodules and chorea, are limited to early life; the tendency of these phenomena to appear independently, scattered singly or in groups through a considerable period; sometimes one, sometimes another, appearing as the primary phase, and the others in varying order of succession; the influence of sex, and of hereditary predisposition, —I pass on to the consideration of the various phases in detail. The first—the arthritis, or articular rheumatism—differs in many notable features from the acute articular rheumatism of later life. I have alluded already to the fact, sufficiently recognised, that the articular affection is usually comparatively slight and may even be absent altogether. It is however, I believe, nearly always present at some period of the rheumatic efflorescence. I have now under my care at St. Mary's Hospital, Kate B——, a girl of fifteen, who was admitted with severe chorea. There was no sign of articular affection, or of any other condition suggestive of rheumatism. The heart's sounds were clear and natural. There was no history of any previous rheumatic affection of any kind to be obtained by most careful inquiry, there was no history of rheumatism of any form in the family, and the case was put down as an instance of non-rheumatic chorea. Twelve days after admission, however, she suddenly complained of pain and stiffness of the right wrist and back of the hand, which were found to be slightly but unmistakably swollen and tender. The arthritis subsided in forty-eight hours. Three days later a similar pain and tenderness of the right wrist and hand developed, subsiding as quickly as the first. It would certainly have escaped serious notice had not my house physician been on the watch for the possible appearance of some rheumatic sign. Such cases give the key to many instances of unexplained heart disease and chorea.[1] The arthritis is,

[1] This has subsequently received further illustration and confirmation. Since the above was written, and three weeks after the occurrence of the transient arthritis above recorded, pericarditis has

indeed, less extreme in every way; there is less swelling and tenderness and pain. It is a comparatively rare thing to see a little child lying still and motionless, bound hand and foot, not daring to move or turn for fear of pain—the condition so characteristic of the disease in an adult. There is often merely a little pain and a little stiffness and tenderness, limited perhaps to a single joint or set of joints, hardly attracting notice, soon forgotten, often overlooked altogether, and constantly never severe enough for the doctor's aid to be called in. It is subsequent heart disease which sends these cases to hospital. Often when medical advice is sought the ailment passes for nothing but a slight feverish attack. Such cases are constantly described as 'low fever.' And, as the inflammatory condition is slight, so many signs met with in severe rheumatic arthritis are wanting. The profuse sweating, the intensely acid, sour-smelling perspiration, which is one of the typical symptoms in the acute rheumatism of adults, is rarely seen in that of children, the rarity being in inverse proportion to age. It only begins to appear with more severe joint affection as age advances, and is rarely extreme before puberty. Other conditions, again,

supervened. The chorea has disappeared, and there is no articular affection.

associated with the profuse sweating are also wanting. The sudamina and miliary eruption which so often accompany it in adults are rarely if ever seen in children. And as the inflammation of joint structures is slight, so also is the pyrexia. The temperature seldom runs high; and this is the more remarkable because, as a rule, it rises readily in children—goes up suddenly for a slight cause to 104° or 105°, perhaps from such trivial disturbance as a dose of irritant food or a passing chill. Moreover, many more structures are involved, so that it must be chiefly arthritis which raises temperature. Yet here, in this eminently pyrexial affection, it seldom rises in children above 101° or 102°; 103° and 104° are comparatively uncommon, and such rise is usually of short duration. Look at the case of S——, for instance, given in Series VIII. As you will see, during his stay in hospital from December, 1887, to March, 1888, a period of four months, he had articular rheumatism, eruption of nodules, endocarditis, and tonsillitis, in addition to chorea and erythema, and died of the disease at last. Yet his temperature was chiefly subnormal, rising only once to 101° for a single night, and once to 100° for a like period. Take, again, the case of John T——, given in Series X. He was in hospital for nine months almost continuously. He had, amongst other rheumatic phases during his stay, arthritis, endocarditis, pericarditis, pleurisy, a pulse of 120 to 130, and the disease steadily progressed to a fatal ending. He died of recurrent pericarditis. Yet his highest temperature was 101·5°; for two short periods only did it reach 101°; for the rest it rarely reached 100°. Hyperpyrexia, which occurs now and again in the acute rheumatism of adults, and is in them so grave and dangerous, often absolutely uncontrollable, is rare in childhood. I have never seen a case of fatal hyperpyrexia in a child, and I can find no instance in which the temperature has shown a persistent tendency to run up rapidly beyond control to a fatal height. Dr. Fagge observed [1] that in fourteen cases of fatal rheumatic hyperpyrexia at Guy's Hospital all but two were over twenty years of age, and these were a boy of nineteen and a girl of eighteen. In Dr. Wilson Fox's [2] twenty-two cases of rheumatic hyperpyrexia the youngest was a girl of seventeen. Dr. Barlow [3] mentions a case of fatal rheumatic hyperpyrexia in a girl of thirteen, but he does not give the range of temperature, or state that hyperpyrexia

---

[1] *Principles and Practice of Medicine*, vol. ii. p. 546.
[2] *Treatment of Hyperpyrexia*, pp. 71–77.
[3] *Brit. Med. Jour.*, September 15, 1883, p. 513.

# EXAMPLES OF ARTHRITIS IN CHILDREN

was the direct cause of death by running up uncontrollably to a fatal height.

The slight arthritis of childhood often assumes a misleading aspect, and it is sometimes difficult to distinguish it from other ailments involving pain and tenderness of parts. Their recognition is of immense importance, since a deadly endocarditis or pericarditis may be insidiously developing concurrently. I give one or two clinical examples of errors of the kind.

M. T——, a girl of three, was observed to be slightly feverish and ailing on February 10. On the 12th the great toe of one foot was found to be swollen and tender. On the 13th she was brought to me. The child had a white and dry tongue; pulse 120; temperature 103°. The swelling and tenderness of the toe were supposed to be due to chilblain. No other joints were affected, but the pulse and temperature suggested articular rheumatism. The heart-sounds were clear. Two days later (February 15) both feet and ankles were slightly stiff, tender, and swollen, and movement of them was painful; temperature 102°. On examining the heart, a soft murmur was audible at the apex. The following day the pain and stiffness of joints were almost gone; temperature 99°. The cardiac murmur had become full and blowing. This murmur persisted for many weeks, and then gradually disappeared. The father's sister and her child had both had acute rheumatism, and the former pericarditis and mitral valvulitis also.

Take another case I saw in consultation a few years ago—a little girl four years old. The child had had for a week or ten days difficulty in putting the right heel down, and was supposed to have incipient talipes, for which she had been galvanised steadily without result. The difficulty in putting down the heel had subsided, but the child still showed the greatest disinclination to walk. I could find no deformity or distortion, but I found both knees unmistakably swollen and tender, especially the left. The temperature was 100°. It turned out, too, upon inquiry, that the girl had suffered from pains and stiffness in the knees and ankles from time to time for the previous six months; and further, the mother had had rheumatic fever. I had no doubt that the joint trouble was rheumatic. Under salicin and citrate of potash all tenderness and stiffness disappeared, and in a day or two the child was running about as usual.

Here is another example. R. C——, a boy five years old, was brought to me because he had suddenly

# EXAMPLES OF ARTHRITIS IN CHILDREN

become unable to walk when he got out of bed in the morning. He was most reluctant to attempt it, but when made to do so he went on tiptoe with bent knees; any attempt to straighten the knees gave pain. The ham-tendons were rigid and very tender. There was no swelling. The temperature was 103°. The heart's action was much excited, but there was no bruit. It appeared that the mother had had rheumatic fever and acute pericarditis, and examination showed a loud mitral murmur. Salicin was given freely, and in twenty-four hours the stiffness and tenderness had so far declined that the child was able to walk, and the temperature had gone down to 100°.

Another example which I think throws great light upon cases of valvular disease of the heart of unexplained origin is that of Ernest C——, a boy who was admitted into the Children's Hospital with a loud mitral regurgitant murmur, heaving, diffused impulse, bulging præcordia, and other signs of hypertrophy and dilatation. He had never been observed to have any articular affection or chorea, or other sign of rheumatism. There was no family history of rheumatism. Three weeks after admission he suddenly complained of pain in one knee, and could not bear to straighten it or use it in walking. The tendons on each side of the popliteal space and its lower border were found tense, swollen, rigid, and extremely tender. There was a slight rise of temperature. In view of the mitral disease, there could be little doubt that the affection of the knee was rheumatic, and that the valvular disease was likewise the result of rheumatic endocarditis, possibly accompanied by some slight arthritis which had escaped with little notice and long been forgotten. This affection of the tendons of the hamstring muscles —the biceps, semi-tendinosus, semi-membranosus, gracilis, and sartorius,—and walking with bent knees on the tips of the toe to avoid tension of them, is, I think, very characteristic. I have seen it now many times in rheumatic children, and it is analogous to the stiff neck and torticollis which is sometimes in like manner the first or sole feature of a rheumatic attack. Conversely, other conditions are often mistaken for articular rheumatism. Essential paralysis in its early stage, when there is great hyperæsthesia, is one of them. The chief points of distinction are that in essential paralysis there is extreme flaccidity of muscle, the limb falling limp and loose, drooping of the toes, and the fact that the tenderness in general is not confined to joints and tendons. Later the disappearance of faradic contractility and tendon reflex would be decisive. I have, however, now under my care at Great Ormond Street a boy who had considerable rigidity about the knees, the extension of which gave great pain. The tenderness was, however, general, the toes drooped, and faradic contractility had almost disappeared in the affected muscles.

Another condition which is liable to be mistaken for slight rheumatic arthritis is syphilitic disease of the ends of the long bones. In this there are tenderness and swelling from accompanying periostitis, and there may be even some arthritis, the limbs being kept motionless from pain on movement. It may be distinguished by the presence of other signs of congenital syphilis, and by the history possibly; but the age at which it occurs—viz. in the first few months after birth—is almost diagnostic. Rheumatic arthritis is almost, if not quite, unknown in early infancy. I have never seen it under two years, although Dr. Goodhart has noted some doubtful cases in children of two or three months, and Henoch records one at ten months. Senator has collected several cases in infants, one at four weeks old.

Another condition which has been mistakenly regarded as rheumatic is the tenderness, swelling, and immobility of the limbs which arise in infantile scurvy

—the so-called scurvy-rickets. This is to be distinguished by the swellings being limited usually to the shafts of the long bones, although I have once seen a periosteal swelling on the malar bone and swelling and tenderness of the joints. Such, however, are rare exceptions. Other diagnostic points are the existence of spongy gums, subcutaneous hæmorrhages, and albuminuria. And then infantile scurvy is limited to the bottle-feeding period—i.e. the first eighteen months or two years, when articular rheumatism is almost unknown. The swelling of the wrists in tetany, the arthritic hæmorrhages of hæmophilia, the joint trouble of strumous disease, and pyæmic arthritis, are all conditions liable to be mistaken for articular rheumatism. I have only time to call attention to them as possible sources of error.

## LECTURE II.

The Anæmia of Rheumatism—Tonsillitis, its relation to rheumatism—Erythema exudativum—Erythema nodosum—Purpura rheumatica—Chorea, its place in the rheumatic series—Subcutaneous nodules, their character and structure—Mode of evolution—Rare in adult life—Pathological and clinical significance—Pleurisy—Occurs in two distinct ways: (1) late, in relation to cardiac disease, as a result of mechanical congestion; and (2) as a primary manifestation of rheumatism.

*Anæmia.*—The effect of rheumatism in producing anæmia in adults is sufficiently well known, but in children this is still more remarkable; the extreme pallor and the hæmic murmurs are often most notable. Dr. Goodhart[1] thinks, further, that even children of rheumatic parentage are often habitually anæmic. Others, again, have regarded anæmia as a predisposing cause of rheumatism. It may be that the inherited rheumatic taint gives the tendency to anæmia, and thus the rheumatism is the antecedent of the anæmia, not the anæmia of the rheumatism. Be this as it may, however, where the rheumatic state

[1] *Diseases of Children*, p. 515.

is actively developed, anæmia proceeds apace in children. The presence of the rheumatic poison appears to be inimical to the red corpuscles or their hæmatin; it either promotes their disintegration or interferes with their production. Trousseau[1] affirms that there is, perhaps, no acute disease which produces anæmia so rapidly as rheumatism; but this is not so. The rheumatic poison is not so rapidly destructive of red blood as that of diphtheria, which causes marked blanching in the course of a few days; but still its effect is decided and unmistakable. This influence of rheumatism in producing anæmia is greatly aggravated when it is accompanied by valvular disease of the heart and pericarditis. The deficient circulation through the lungs—the deficient oxygenation—may, in part, account for this; and it is accompanied, also, by progressive emaciation. Of this, however, I shall speak in the concluding lecture. I have now under my care a child with chorea and pericarditis. There is no arthritis, but the patient has had articular rheumatism before. The anæmia is extreme; the pallor that of a marked chlorosis.

*Tonsillitis.*—The claim of tonsillitis to be ranked as one of the rheumatic series is, I think, well established. Tonsillitis is a common disorder, and

[1] *Clin. Med.*, vol. iv. p. 454.

often arises independently; but it occurs so frequently in direct and immediate association with articular rheumatism that some pathological connection cannot be doubted. Trousseau [1] recognised a rheumatic sore-throat, and showed how this was apt to alternate at one time with stiff neck and torticollis, at another with joint pain and lumbago. Attention was again drawn to the almost forgotten observation of Trousseau by Dr. Kingston Fowler [2] in 1880, who published an account of twenty cases of acute rheumatism ushered in by tonsillitis. The statistics of the Collective Investigation Committee [3] show that tonsillitis was associated with rheumatism in 158 cases out of 655, or 24·12 per cent., in addition to twenty cases of sore-throat, the exact nature of which was not described. If these were added the proportion would be 27·17 per cent.[4] It is assumed, I think, generally, that tonsillitis always precedes the articular affection, and usually comes immediately before it— ushers it in, as the phrase goes; and this is no doubt the rule, but it is by no means invariable. Tonsillitis may occur at any period of the rheumatic series, although most often it comes first—immediately

---

[1] *Clin. Med.* vol. ii. p. 466.   [2] *Lancet*, December 11, 1880.
[3] *Brit. Med. Jour.*: Dr. Whipham's Report, Feb. 25, 1888, p. 391.
[4] Dr. Fowler estimated it as occurring in 80 per cent. of cases.

preceding arthritis.[1] In all but three of the 158 cases just quoted the tonsillitis preceded the arthritis at various intervals; in two of the remaining three cases the tonsillitis accompanied the joint affection, and in the third followed it. In the fatal case of W. S——, shown in Series VIII., it came last of all. In the case of William K——, a boy of eight, recently under my care, it likewise occurred last of a series beginning with arthritis and endocarditis; four months later, chorea; at the close of the chorea, acute tonsillitis. My own boy, of whose case I have spoken as having exhibited almost all the phases of rheumatism except carditis, had tonsillitis during the period of arthritis, and constant, repeated, and severe attacks during the period of chorea, and for a considerable term after all other signs of rheumatism had ceased. Of four other children, not one has suffered from tonsillitis, although all have been brought up together under like conditions. Whether the tonsillitis set up by rheumatism presents any distinctive characters, I cannot say with certainty. Trousseau affirmed that it could be distinguished by its ephemeral character, lasting only from thirty to

[1] Dr. Archibald Garrod and Mr. Cooke, in a paper published in the *Lancet*, July 21, 1888, found the percentage of cases of tonsillitis with rheumatic family history exactly the same as the percentage of articular rheumatism with rheumatic history—viz. 35 per cent.

forty-eight hours, and he describes the rheumatic sore-throat as something more than tonsillitis, involving the pharynx, soft palate, and uvula. In some cases which I have observed, the diffused character of the inflammatory redness and swelling was very marked; but I do not know that this is invariable; further observation is needed on this point. It is probable that tonsillitis may occur as a solitary expression of the rheumatic state. In many cases it arises in rheumatic subjects quite apart from the articular manifestation. Of its concurrence with another rheumatic affection—viz. chorea—I have seen three examples quite recently, and in all these the chorea occurred in a child who had articular rheumatism at another epoch. But of its connection with endocarditis or pericarditis apart from arthritis I have no certain knowledge.[1] Tonsillitis

[1] I have not traced the connection; but, curiously enough, as I was in the act of writing this portion of my lecture I was asked by Mr. Kiallmark to see, in consultation with him, a little boy of six suffering from relapsing tonsillitis, in whom he had discovered, to his dismay, a distinct apex murmur. The child had had previous attacks, and Mr. Kiallmark had judged them to be rheumatic. The boy has had no arthritis, and there is no distinct rheumatic family history. The tonsillitis rapidly got well under salicylate of soda, recurring three times when this medicine was omitted. The murmur is a soft one, audible over the tricuspid area, not at the apex. I am doubtful whether it is organic, but I shall be much interested to learn its future course.

is set up by many other causes as well as by rheumatism. The decision whether a given case of tonsillitis not immediately associated with articular rheumatism is of rheumatic nature must be based upon a comprehensive survey of the patient's life history and family predisposition, as well as of the accompanying symptoms. If it occurs in a child with a strong family history of acute rheumatism, or in one who has had articular affection, this is presumptive evidence in favour of the tonsillitis being rheumatic. Even if there has been no arthritis at any time, the concurrence of other members of the rheumatic series—such as subcutaneous nodules, chorea, endocarditis, pericarditis, or erythema—would afford evidence weighty in proportion to the particular phases developed, the completeness of the combination, and the extent of the series.

*Erythema exudativum.*—The connection of erythema exudativum with the rheumatic state appears much more clearly in the case of children than of adults. With the latter it occurs occasionally; with children, according to my experience, it is common. The statistics of the Collective Investigation Committee give only thirty-two cases out of 655, or not quite 5 per cent.; but these contain very few children—only fifty-one under twelve. Dr. Barlow and

Dr. Warner found that, of twenty-seven patients with rheumatic nodules, eight had erythema papulatum or marginatum, one urticaria, and one purpura—i.e. ten out of twenty-seven, and these in close association with the evolution of the nodules. It appears in various forms—erythema marginatum, erythema papulatum, erythema nodosum, and urticaria, the first named being the most common. The erythema may occur at any point in the rheumatic series; but it is usually, at any rate, associated with the development of active rheumatic disturbance of some other kind, and occurs chiefly in the marginate or urticarious form. These varieties are not unfrequently associated with endocarditis and pericarditis in the more serious cases. In eight cases of extreme gravity which have come under my care within the last year, four of which were fatal from persistent recurrent pericarditis and endocarditis, erythema of this kind occurred in one-half—two of the fatal cases and two others. Dr. Barlow, in his excellent introduction to the discussion of rheumatism at the meeting of the British Medical Association at Liverpool in 1883, refers to a case under his observation in which erythema occurred as one of a group in the rheumatic series, associated with endocarditis, pleurisy, and pneumonia, but without arthritis; the arthritis had occurred years before. He mentions another case, also under his own observation, where erythema appeared as one of a group of rheumatic phenomena, which included nodules, chorea, and fatal pericarditis, but no arthritis; that had occurred in a previous explosion of rheumatic activity. Dr. Barlow also gives two other cases in which exudative erythema ushered in rheumatic seizures—including endocarditis and pericarditis, with arthritis following.

With regard to the special form erythema nodosum, it would appear that, although it has, so to speak, an arthritis of its own, it is associated sometimes with true articular rheumatism. The eruption is attended in itself with pain of joints, and sometimes swelling, possibly from pressure. But it also arises in connection with genuine acute articular rheumatism. Sir Thomas Watson observed it to occur both before and after this affection, and quotes Rayer as having seen it in the same connection. I have just had under my care, in Great Ormond Street, a case which is interesting as illustrating the rheumatic connection, the concurrence of endocarditis, and also the occurrence of this eruption at an early age. Walter G——, aged two years and eight months, was admitted on October 1 last with well-marked erythema nodosum on both shins. There was no arthritis, or any history of its previous occurrence at any period, yet the child has a well-marked mitral regurgitant murmur, undoubtedly organic. The father had had 'rheumatism,' and the father's sister rheumatic fever twice.[1] The tendency of erythema nodosum to occur especially in young girls—who are also most liable to rheumatic arthritis, to endocarditis, and to chorea —is in agreement with the view of its rheumatic nature; yet exudative erythema, although often rheumatic, is, like arthritis and tonsillitis, set up by other causes than rheumatism. The facts that erythema occurs in cholera and in septicæmia as the result of poisoning by certain drugs, and the urticarious form by food-poisoning, suggest a similar influence of the rheumatic poison, and we should look at the appearance of erythema in any given case as probably indicative of the existence of some irritant matter which is in circulation acting either directly or by reflection upon the skin. Such irritant may be the rheumatic virus; whether it is so or not must be determined by careful examination

---

[1] Since the above was written I have met with an instance of erythema nodosum occurring together with subcutaneous tendinous nodules, apart from any other rheumatic manifestation except tonsillitis (F. V—— æt. $8\frac{1}{2}$, St. Mary's Hosp., Feb. 1889).

of the evidence afforded by the presence or absence of other members of the rheumatic series, or by their previous occurrence, together with the existence or otherwise of family predisposition.

*Purpura rheumatica.*—This appears especially in rheumatic subjects, and, like erythema nodosum, has a local *quasi*-arthritis of its own; when it appears on the legs and ankles, the ankle-joints and feet are swollen, tender, and painful. But it arises also in the course of general acute articular rheumatism, as I have seen more than once; although usually, I think, it occurs independently. In one case, the patient whom I have mentioned before, a boy of eight (Series VII.) had had acute rheumatism severely twelve months before. The eruption appeared after standing about in the wet grass while very hot from playing cricket—a profuse crop of large purpuric spots on both legs, mostly about the ankles. There was much swelling of the ankle-joints, which were so tender that he could not bear to walk or move them; but no other joints were affected, and there were never any constitutional symptoms or the smallest rise of temperature, although it was taken frequently, from apprehension of a second attack of rheumatic fever. From these two circumstances— viz. that the ankles only were attacked, and that there was never any fever or general illness—I conclude the swelling was not directly rheumatic, but a local œdema, from purpuric extravasation or thrombosis of venules. Purpura rheumatica, then, while sometimes concurrent with active, acute, articular rheumatism, occurs also apart from it in rheumatic subjects, and is probably a minor expression of the rheumatic state, although far less common than exudative erythema.

*Chorea.*—This is one of the most interesting members of the rheumatic series. When associated with articular rheumatism it usually follows the arthritis; it is sometimes concurrent with it; and sometimes, again, as I have shown, and as M. Roger noted long ago, it precedes the joint affection. Instances of this are shown in the clinical examples given in the preceding lecture. Chorea has furnished several curious pathological problems, which have given rise to frequent discussions and controversies, some of which continue to rage unsettled to this day. All are agreed, I think, that there is a certain connection between chorea and rheumatism. As Dr. Barlow has well observed, there is no other general disease or fever of childhood with which chorea has any such association, with the single exception of scarlet fever, and that in far less degree; and scarlet fever, significantly enough, is the one fever especially associated with acute rheumatism. We never see a measles chorea, or a whooping-cough chorea, or a mumps chorea. The only points in dispute, then, are the nature of such relation between chorea and rheumatism, and its closeness and constancy. Some hold with M. Roger that all chorea is rheumatic—that it owns no other source; others that the relation is comparatively slight and rare. Statistics have been supplied on each side, some supporting one view, some another, varying perhaps in degree according to the unconscious bias of the compiler. Let me state clearly my own position on this question. I do not think the evidence warrants the assumption that chorea is invariably of rheumatic origin. I must say of chorea, as of tonsillitis, erythema, endocarditis, pericarditis, and arthritis—in fact, of the whole of the rheumatic series except subcutaneous nodules—that it is produced by other causes as well as by rheumatism. But I am convinced that rheumatism is the most common and potent factor. Other factors, however, must be taken into account in forming any satisfactory explanation of the genesis of chorea. There is a physiological basis in that greater mobility of nervous system and motor readiness of expression so well described by Dr. Sturges, and in the more excitable temperament of quick, intelligent children, and of girls as compared with boys. This all tells and plays a part in the development of chorea. Yet it is singular how small the association with other neuroses appears to be, at any rate as far as the individuals are concerned; for these are found, according to the Statistics of the Collective Investigation Committee,[1] in 97 cases only out of 439, or a little more than 22 per cent., and these 97 include 79 cases of headache and migraine, so that if there is any pathological affinity it is with those special forms only. Taking the question of inheritance, there is what is termed a neurotic family history in no less than 46 per cent. At first sight this seems significant, but on examination the neurotic affections included are such a motley crew that their presence in the record does not carry much weight; for the list embraces paralysis, drunkenness, tubercular meningitis, diabetes, sunstroke, spinal injury, and sciatica. There is not, as might fairly have been expected, a large proportion of hysteria (7·5 per cent.) The only connection which comes out with any significance is chorea itself (14 per cent.), and this probably represents a rheumatic as much as a neurotic relation. And while I am upon this subject, let me pause for

[1] *Coll. Invest. Record,* vol. iii. p. 54.

a moment to explode a time-honoured fallacy in the etiology of chorea—that is, that it spreads by imitation. This was true of the dancing mania of the middle ages, which spread amongst enthusiasts by a sort of hysterical contagion. And children learn certain tricks of grimacing. But they never acquire true chorea by imitation any more than they acquire nodules, or paresis, or endocarditis by imitation. Dr. West,[1] indeed, speaks of it as occurring occasionally, and of the necessity arising for changing the position of patients, to prevent the involuntary mimicry by one child of the movements of another. In the Collective Investigation Report[2] two cases are recorded as mimetic, but no details are given. I have now been connected with the hospital in Great Ormond Street for some twenty years. Cases of chorea are extremely common there; in the girls' wards, especially, there are often five or six or more cases at a time. It is very rarely, indeed, that there are not some. They are placed indiscriminately with other children, and yet I have not seen a single instance of its spread by imitation. I believe the separation of children to prevent mimetic development of chorea is entirely unnecessary. The belief

[1] *Diseases of Infancy and Childhood*, seventh edition, p. 236.
[2] Vol. iii. p. 48.

in its production in this way is a survival of some old tradition, or has arisen from mistaking a trick of grimacing for true chorea. The statement has got into text-books, and, like many other time-honoured fallacies, holds its ground there, simply because it is taken for granted without inquiry. In speaking of grimacing, I may here also allude, in passing, to the minor chorea, which consists in mere winking of the eye and twitching of the lips or nose, without jactitation of the limbs. This is, I believe, usually a local chorea, connected with the eruption of the second teeth, and especially of the eye-teeth, and not, I think, essentially connected with rheumatism.

Now taking true chorea, there is, even in the rheumatic cases, often something more than the constitutional basis of mobility of the nervous system, influenced and played upon by the rheumatic poison. There is frequently another factor—nervous shock. Sometimes the rheumatic invasion seems to be the direct exciting cause, as well as the predisposing influence; when, for instance, as often happens, chorea immediately follows or is concurrent with articular rheumatism, and endocarditis or pericarditis. But shock or mental excitement is frequently found as the immediate exciting cause of the choreic disturbance in rheumatic subjects. Witness the case of J. T——, Series X., eminently rheumatic, yet having two attacks of chorea ascribed to fright long before the first arthritis; and this shock or excitement is a common exciting cause enough in rheumatic cases. A remarkable instance of the effect of mental excitement came under my observation a year or two ago in a case of rheumatic chorea. A little girl of eight years old had acute rheumatism, with endocarditis and pericarditis, and followed immediately by severe chorea. The chorea got absolutely well in the course of a few weeks, and the child was brought up to London for change. She was taken to the pantomime for the first time, and became wildly excited. The next morning I was sent for to see her; chorea had returned so violently that she had to be held by her mother and nurse to keep her falling from the bed. I have never seen more extreme jactitation. This happened instantly in a single night. And, again, a public schoolboy under my care for chorea following articular rheumatism, on his recovery returned to school and to work. His chorea did not return until he got into a quarrel and scuffle with another boy. The next day he was again choreic as before. I would insist on the fact that there is nothing antagonistic between the agency of nervous shock or excitement and

## RELATION OF CHOREA TO RHEUMATISM

rheumatism. They are concerned together as factors in many cases of chorea, as in the two examples just quoted. Yet fright chorea and rheumatic chorea are spoken of as if distinct. If fright is the immediate exciting cause in a given case it is labelled 'fright chorea,' as distinguished from rheumatic chorea. Such distinction is fallacious and misleading, and has confused the etiology of chorea. The rheumatic state is the most common predisposing cause. Sometimes the choreic disturbance follows on this without obvious immediate exciting cause. Often a nervous shock stirs it suddenly into action; fright acts equally on rheumatic and non-rheumatic.

Turning now to the vexed question of the degree of closeness and constancy of the connection between chorea and rheumatism, I would point out that the only evidence dealt with by most writers on the subject is the occurrence of acute articular rheumatism either preceding or accompanying the chorea. But there is a great deal of evidence in addition, some of it of quite recent development, which bears upon the question; this cannot be ignored; it must at least be taken into consideration and duly weighed in order to come to a correct judgment in the matter. Let me indicate some of these neglected data. In the first place, it appears from the Statistics of the

Collective Investigation Committee, as previously stated, that between the ages of ten and fifteen, girls have a remarkable proclivity to acute articular rheumatism as compared with boys during the same period, which is that of the maximum incidence of chorea. This corresponds with a similar greater proclivity during that same period of girls as compared with boys to organic heart-disease associated with acute rheumatism, to organic heart-disease associated with chorea, and to articular rheumatism associated with chorea. The special proclivity of girls to chorea is more protracted, extending throughout childhood and adolescence. This singular harmony of relative incidence of these affections upon the sexes is possibly capable of more than one interpretation, but it is *primâ facie* very suggestive of a close pathological connection.[1]

Further, there is the evidence of arthritis occur-

[1] Collating the cases given in the Collective Investigation Record, it appears (Tables of Cases, vol. iv.) that, for this period of eleven to fifteen, acute articular rheumatism is met with in girls as compared with boys as 47 to 25, or nearly 2 to 1 ; rheumatic heart-disease in about the same proportion—viz. 28 to 16, or nearly 2 to 1. Chorea associated with antecedent or concurrent articular rheumatism occurs in girls as compared with boys in still higher proportion—viz. 116 to 32 (vol. xiv. p. 47), or more than 3 to 1 ; organic heart-disease in connection with chorea (collated from cases in vol. iii.) also in greater proportion—viz. 43 to 13, or more than 3 to 1 ; chorea generally, 131 to 47, or not quite 3 to 1 (vol. iii. p. 47).

ring after the chorea. This is by far the least common sequence. The proportion is not large, yet, according to my observation, much more than indicated by the thirteen instances out of 655 cases of rheumatism furnished by the Collective Investigation Record. Of these, nine are under the age of nineteen; three, twenty-four; one, twenty-seven. The explanation lies probably partly in the fact that these cases comprise a singularly small proportion of children. A considerable number of children with rheumatic chorea must be carried off by heart-disease before reaching maturity, and those who survive are forgetful of slight choreas which are usually classed as fidgetiness or nervousness.[1] Be this as it may, however, there are a certain number of cases of chorea connected with rheumatism usually excluded from the estimate.

Then, again, there is the evidence afforded by the association of chorea with other conditions which are themselves found in close relation to articular rheumatism—i.e. the other members of the rheumatic series. This evidence is of weight cumulative

[1] That this is so I have many times had proof from private cases—children brought for nervousness and restlessness, who on examination turn out to have the jactitations of slight chorea. These cases do not come into hospital, and amongst the poor they probably never come under the observation of a doctor.

in proportion to the number and importance of the phases combined. Thus the occurrence of endocarditis or pericarditis in association with chorea would have a certain significance. When a case of endocarditis or pericarditis arises in connection with chorea, even if there be no arthritis, since rheumatism is the chief cause of endocarditis and pericarditis on the one hand, and so closely associated with chorea, on the other, the concurrence of these—each *per se* allowed to be frequently rheumatic—affords a considerable presumption that they are together rheumatic. There is no other general morbid state so closely associated with chorea as rheumatism. There are only two diseases largely and closely associated with endocarditis—viz. chorea and rheumatism. Explanations, more or less plausible, have been suggested as to the cause of the endocarditis of chorea apart from rheumatism. But no dynamic theory will explain the *pericarditis* of chorea when it occurs without articular affection. The significance of this fact has, I think, been overlooked.

The association of erythema nodosum or tonsillitis with the endocarditis or pericarditis would greatly strengthen the presumption of the rheumatic nature of an accompanying chorea; while the presence of nodules, so absolutely associated with rheumatic activity, would be in itself, I think, conclusive. The recent recognition of the rheumatic relations of the exudative erythemata and nodules has, indeed, brought much new light, and the evidence which these affections afford has yet to be fully collected and appraised. The history of a strong family predisposition to rheumatism, again, would possess a certain value. Look at the case of W. S—— in Series VIII., and that of J. T—— in Series X. In both these, as I pointed out previously, the chorea occurred long before the joint affection; and there was nothing to identify it as rheumatic at the time it occurred except the accompanying endocarditis, and in the latter case the fact that the child's mother had had rheumatic fever; yet later came the fatal series of events stamping it as rheumatic—the endocarditis, pericarditis, nodules, and arthritis.

Two days ago I saw a boy of eight (Charles B——),[1] the child of well-to-do people, who had general chorea of moderate intensity. He had never had arthritis, he had no nodules, and there was no sign of cardiac affection. I learnt, however, from the boy's mother, a young woman, that she suffered frequently from painful swelling of the finger-joints; that her brother, a young man of thirty, suffered

[1] Notebook XIII. p. 467.

from valvular disease of the heart, on account of which he had been refused for life assurance; that her mother and two of her mother's sisters suffered from subacute rheumatism, and another of her mother's sisters had had rheumatic fever. No neurotic taint of any kind could be made out. Does not such a history afford at least a presumption that the chorea known to be so often rheumatic owed something to the rheumatic connection in this instance? It is, moreover, to be noted that this history was only elicited by careful cross-examination. The answer to my first question, as to whether there was rheumatism in the family, was in the negative. Had I been content with it I should have failed to trace the rheumatic taint.

Another case (D. D——)[1] now under my care is more suggestive—a little girl of four, brought to me for a slight general chorea. She had never had articular rheumatism. There were no nodules to be found, and the heart's sounds were normal. On inquiry I learnt that the mother's sister had had rheumatic fever and severe chorea; her mother had had rheumatic fever, and died of heart disease. Does not such a history raise a strong presumption of the rheumatic connection in the child's chorea?

[1] Notebook XIV. p. 7.

Again, I have this week received into the Children's Hospital a boy of five, with chorea and small nodules. He has no arthritis, apparently no fresh endocarditis. The pulse is quiet; the temperature normal. The only sign of rheumatic activity is the development of the nodules, and with it the chorea. Yet he had rheumatic arthritis more than ten months ago, and has a double mitral murmur.

Take, again, the case of H. C——, Series IV. He had chorea in 1875, accompanied no doubt by endocarditis, for he was admitted with advanced mitral disease in 1878. He had never had arthritis as far as was known. But his mother had had rheumatic fever and mitral disease. Is it not probable, to say the least of it, that the endocarditis and chorea were both rheumatic, the arthritis possibly having occurred without being noticed, or being yet to follow (as we have seen it sometimes do) later in the series?

Evidence of this kind must be taken into account, although it is difficult to estimate it statistically. When all these considerations which I have pointed out have been allowed due weight, there remains still a certain proportion of cases in which no rheumatic connection of any kind can be traced. The unsettled question is as to its measure and degree. Various estimates have been made. The value of such estimation is, to my mind, very doubtful. In most instances the data are very imperfect. We may, I think, for example, at once put aside as inadequate all statistics based—as nearly the whole of them are—solely upon antecedent attacks of well-marked articular rheumatism, since they take into account only one phase, in severe form, occurring previously or concurrent with the chorea. Such statistics are necessarily defective, because—1. They omit many slight cases of joint or tendon affection such as those of which I gave examples in the first lecture, conditions constantly unnoticed or forgotten, or, if observed, not regarded as rheumatic.[1] 2. They omit all cases in which the joint affection comes after the chorea. 3. They fail to take into account all the evidence afforded by the occurrence and concurrence of subcutaneous nodules, of endocarditis, of

[1] It is significant, in relation to the genuine rheumatic character of so-called growing pains, that a family history of rheumatism is found in 49 per cent. of all 'vague pains,' almost identical with the 52 per cent. in definite acute articular rheumatism, and more than double the percentage found in diseases of all kinds, as stated by Dr. Sturges and Dr. Archibald Garrod—viz. 20 per cent. (*Collective Investigation Record*, vol. iii. p. 48). The case of Kate B——, given in the first lecture, illustrates this point also. She was admitted for chorea. No history of articular rheumatism either in the patient or her family could be obtained, and the case was recorded as one of non-rheumatic chorea. Twelve days later she developed slight arthritis, lasting forty-eight hours. Three weeks later still pericarditis appeared, the articular affection and chorea having entirely ceased.

pericarditis, of erythema, and of tonsillitis ; so that, unless well-marked articular rheumatism has likewise occurred before the chorea, these are classed as non-rheumatic. 4. They omit to take into account the evidence afforded by family predisposition. The latest important statistics, those of the Collective Investigation Committee, likewise necessarily underestimate the rheumatic element, although in less degree. They do, indeed, take into account not only previous acute articular rheumatism, but also those cases in which it accompanied the chorea or followed it immediately. But by the very nature of the case, being a report on chorea at the time, they do not take into account cases where the joint affection occurs some time afterwards, and apart from the chorea. Many cases, again (slight joint affections, not being identified as rheumatic by the observers), are probably classed as 'vague pains.' Many, again, are no doubt altogether overlooked. Moreover, in these statistics, as in others, the significance of mitral disease, of erythema, of tonsillitis, and of nodules, alone or in combination, is not estimated or admitted into the rheumatic proof; and how little this most important and common piece of evidence, the evolution of nodules, is looked for and recognised, and how wanting these statistics must be in this respect, appears from the fact that, of 439 cases of chorea recorded, in only seven instances were nodules observed. Why, we have sometimes as many in the wards at Great Ormond Street at the same time! There are six at the present moment. The statistics of the Collective Investigation Committee, based upon this single rheumatic event of articular affection before, during, or immediately after the event, give a 32 percentage of chorea positively rheumatic. If to these be added the cases of vague pains the percentage is 46·2. The estimates of two of the most sagacious clinical observers of our time come near to this. Dr. Stephen Mackenzie found 44·76 per cent. almost certainly rheumatic, and, for reasons similar to those I have put forward, he regards this as representing very imperfectly the rheumatic connection of chorea. Dr. Barlow finds in forty-four out of seventy-three, or 60 per cent., sufficient evidence of rheumatism, and points out that the existence of progressive heart-disease and the imperfection of the record render it probable that many other cases should be included. In eighty-four cases minutely recorded and specially investigated by myself, I find satisfactory evidence of acute rheumatism in the patient or immediate relatives in sixty-two—i.e. in 75 per cent. Leaving out the family history, the estimate would coincide very closely with that of Dr. Barlow. It may, then, I think, be concluded that in the majority of cases at least chorea is a phase of rheumatism.

It is not my purpose to enter into the question of the minute morbid anatomy of chorea, or the exact mechanism by which the motor disturbance is effected —whether by embolism in the motor tract, or by thrombosis there, or the irritant effect of the rheumatic virus, or the mysterious influence of nervous shock. All these in the present state of precise pathological knowledge can only be matters of speculation. But I may point to the possibility of some proliferative change in the neuroglia akin to that of the fibrous tissues elsewhere as a point which needs examination.

Before leaving the subject of chorea, however, I should like to call attention to the relation of nervous excitability to rheumatism. The rheumatic children who develop chorea are intellectual, highly strung, excitable, and nervous, often emotional, just as other choreic children. The question arises, is the nervous instability due to the influence of the recent active rheumatic state induced by it? The extraordinary emotional attacks observed in some cases of rheumatic chorea (as in the examples of W. S——,

Series VIII., and J. T——, Series X.) would favour this. Or is the nervous instability part of the original constitution of the child, and chorea produced when this is acted upon by a second factor—viz. rheumatism? Or do the two tendencies run together in the original diathesis?—the child with a tendency to rheumatism inheriting therewith a mobile nervous system, as suggested by Sir Dyce Duckworth.[1] I am inclined to think the latter: that nervous excitability goes with the rheumatic diathesis, and that it is stirred up to active eruption of motor disturbance in chorea by some direct exciting cause—fright, or acute rheumatism, or pregnancy. I have seen this excitable tendency in the single child of a family in many instances. The rheumatic child is the excitable, emotional child. The rheumatic tendency and the nervous excitability run together in the same inherited constitution or diathesis.

*Subcutaneous Tendinous Nodules.*—I now turn to the next phase or manifestation—viz. the evolution of subcutaneous nodules. The actual discovery of these nodules is no new thing. They were observed by Hillier, who gives an excellent account of a typical case in his book on the Diseases of Children,

---

[1] Address to the Thames Valley Branch of the British Medical Association at Richmond (*Brit. Med. Jour.* Jan. 3, 1885).

published in 1868. The case was one of chorea with pyrexia and organic mitral murmur, but no articular rheumatism. Cases have since been reported by Meynet and others. I had long been familiar with them as occurring occasionally in the course of articular rheumatism; but the credit of pointing out their frequency and great importance as clinical signs in the various manifestations of rheumatism belongs to Dr. Barlow and Dr. Warner.[1] These fibrous nodules are common in children—much more rare in adults. I have seen only two cases in adults, scores in children. This is perhaps partly the reason why they have not been more frequently observed, for we take our ideas of rheumatism from the disease as seen in adults. A second reason why they are not observed is that they are not known or looked for; and a third reason why they often escape notice is their small size in many cases. They are sometimes to be felt rather than seen. In one case now under my observation, two of these growths, the size of a hempseed, on the tendons of the outer malleolus, only become visible when the skin is drawn tightly over them, although they can be detected readily enough by touch. In the 655 cases of articular

---

[1] *Trans. Int. Med. Cong.* 1881, vol. iv.

rheumatism given in the Collective Investigation Record (vol. iv.), there are only thirty-six in which nodules are recorded. Of these only five are in children under sixteen; but then the returns embrace a very small proportion of children. The chorea returns [1] yield only twelve cases out of 439. Yet I have at the present moment five under my care in hospital, and there are two more under my colleagues; all these are, except one of articular rheumatism, cases of chorea. The nodules vary in size, from that of a hempseed to that of an almond or larger; in extreme instances they may attain that of half a walnut, as in the case of W. S——, Series VIII. (represented in the coloured illustration), and also in that of J. T——, Series X., and some others. The nodules lie under the skin, and are connected with fascia or tendons—in relation with fibrous tissues. They are not tender, except slightly in rare instances. There is no redness of the skin over them, except occasionally from friction or pressure. They are found most commonly upon the back of the elbow, over the malleoli, and at the margin of the patella. They are also found not unfrequently upon the head, especially along the superior curved line of the occiput, the temporal ridge, and now and

[1] *Coll. Invest. Record*, vol. iii.

again upon the extensor and flexor surfaces of the hands, on the extensors of the feet, the vertebral spines, the spine of the scapula, and the crista ilii. In extrême cases—as in that of W. S——, nodules may be found in nearly all these positions. Once I have seen them the size of almonds studded over the flexor tendons on the palms of the hands, and once in great numbers over the tendinous structures of the intercostals, on the front and sides of the thorax. There may be only one of these nodules, but more usually three or four are to be found; sometimes the number is large, as many as thirty or forty. I have counted thirty-five at one time. Sometimes there is only a single crop; sometimes several crops appear in succession. These fibrous growths are developed to perceptible size in the course of a few days; I have, for example, been unable to find one anywhere at one hospital visit, and have discovered several at the next, three days later. The large nodules, however, take a considerable period to attain their full dimensions. Their duration varies from a few days to several months. The shortest time I have noted is fourteen days, but Dr. Barlow [1] observed one to come and disappear again in three days. Large nodules—such as those of W. S——

[1] *Trans. Int. Med. Cong.* 1881, vol. iv.

shown in the Plate—have an existence of months. Dr. Barlow has recorded their persistence for five months. The evolution of the nodules in itself gives rise to no pain or fever. If this be present, it is due to concurrent arthritis, or cardiac inflammation, or pleurisy. For example, in the case of two children under my care, in whom nodules have developed in conjunction with chorea, the temperature has never been above normal. When the nodular growths are exposed by dissection, they appear as 'oval semi-transparent fibrous bodies, like boiled sago-grains.'[1] Examined microscopically in thin section, they exhibit wavy bands of tissue, with caudate and spindle-shaped cells and abundant nuclear growth, and they are highly vascular. They consist, therefore, of nuclear growth in process of development into fibrous tissue in all stages of transformation. These appearances are shown in the section under the microscope, for which I am indebted to Mr. Priestley, the registrar to the Children's Hospital, and are represented in the drawings given in the next lecture. A subcutaneous nodule is a proliferation of fibrous tissue, just such as that developed in the interstitial framework of the liver or in the nerve-sheaths by undue stimulation

[1] *Trans. Int. Med. Cong.* 1881, vol. iv.

of alcoholic or other irritation. As Dr. Dickinson has well said,[1] the tissues of a child, and especially the fibrous tissues, are more readily excited to sprout in this way than those of adults, as shown by the rapid growth of fibrous tissue in hypertrophic cirrhosis and interstitial nephritis in children; the quick hypertrophy of muscle in cardiac disease and the marvellous growth of sarcomatous tumours are analogous examples. On this point I shall have more to say in the next lecture, when I come to speak of endocarditis and pericarditis.

The connection of these nodules with rheumatism is extremely close, and I believe absolute. As far as I can judge, they own no other origin or connection. In all cases in which I have seen them, there has been either rheumatic joint affection at the time or at some period of the child's history, or such a concurrence of rheumatic events, one or more—such as endocarditis, pericarditis, chorea, and erythema— that there could be no doubt as to the nature of the condition. In nineteen out of twenty-seven cases recorded by Dr. Barlow there was arthritis; in six more there was distinct joint pain, and other evidence of the rheumatic state. In nearly every case

[1] Introductory Address at the Hospital for Sick Children (*Lancet*, November 3, 1888).

recorded by others, the rheumatic connection has been clearly traced. As evidence of rheumatism they are, I think, indisputable. But there is something more than this. Not only are these nodules connected with rheumatism, but they are specially connected with the graver forms of it; and they are signs, serious apparently in proportion to their size and number. Look at the case of W. S—— (Series VIII.) and that of J. T—— (Series X.) What a list of rheumatic events! In the first, repeated endocarditis, chorea, arthritis, and almost certainly pericarditis, accompanied the evolution of nodules. In the second, endocarditis, chorea, pleurisy, and pericarditis. Both cases ended fatally in spite of all treatment. Nothing availed to stop steadily progressive endocarditis and pericarditis. Salicylate of soda, salicin, free doses of alkalies and quinine, and mercurial inunction were equally futile. Of six cases of this kind, where the nodules were numerous and large, which came under my care at the Children's Hospital during the last year, four were fatal. In all cases but one there was chorea. In every one there was endocarditis. In three, and probably in four, there was pericarditis. In two there was pleurisy.

So far as my present experience goes, I regard the eruption of large nodules, such as are shown

## CLINICAL SIGNIFICANCE OF NODULES

in the Plate, as almost equivalent to a sentence of death. They mean persistent cardiac disease, generally uncontrollable, and marching almost infallibly to a fatal ending. General experience agrees as to the grave significance of these fibrous growths, which were at first looked upon as unimportant curiosities. Seven years ago, Dr. Barlow and Dr. Warner[1] recognised their serious import. In every one of the twenty-seven cases observed by them there was organic heart-disease; in eight there was pericarditis; in twelve there was progressive valvular disease; and eight were fatal in spite of all treatment. The forecast has proved correct. Dr. Money, who has since investigated the subject, found nodules in half the cases of rheumatism in which well-marked heart-disease occurred, and my experience is quite in accord with these observations. The cases recorded by others appear to have been almost uniformly severe and frequently fatal. I could give examples of the association of these nodules with every other phase of the rheumatic series, as well as with endocarditis and pericarditis and chorea and pleurisy already mentioned; and in all these cases the evidence they afford as to the rheumatic nature of the affection is of the highest value, and I believe

[1] *Trans. Int. Med. Cong.* 1881, vol. iv.

decisive. But their greatest interest lies in the fact of their frequent association with endocarditis and pericarditis of the most deadly, although subacute form, and in their connection with chorea.

*Pleurisy.*—Pleurisy occurs in association with rheumatism in two distinct ways. It arises frequently towards the end of rheumatic heart-disease —partly, perhaps, as a result of the mechanical congestion of the pleura, caused by the valvular defect, or by pericarditis, or by extension from the latter. Of this late pleurisy, instances are common enough, as in the cases of Series II. and X. Of it I shall say nothing further, since it is probably due as much to cardiac as to primary rheumatic causes. But pleurisy likewise occurs in rheumatism as an initial phenomenon, coming immediately before, together with, or immediately after arthritis, as a direct result of rheumatic influence. It is likely enough that it occurs quite independently, apart from all other phases, yet still a rheumatic manifestation. Probably many of the simple pleurisies and pleuropneumonias we see and regard as idiopathic would be found, on careful inquiry, to be of rheumatic origin. This is a point which deserves further investigation. Cases such as the two following are, however, very suggestive. For the particulars of the first I am indebted to Dr. Lewis, of Hamilton Terrace, with whom I saw the case.

On Dec. 22nd, 1887, a boy of ten travelled up to town from the seaside in extremely bitter weather. On the 24th he complained of pain in the ear, and subsequently had purulent discharge from it. On the 25th he was sick twice. At this point Dr. Lewis saw the boy, and found him with a temperature of 104°, and sweating profusely. No physical signs of any kind could be detected. On the 26th the fever and sweating continued; the temperature was 104·2°. On examination of the chest, pleuritic friction was heard at one spot, and this had greatly extended next day. Three days later he complained of pain and stiffness in the wrists, knees, and ankles, which were discovered to be swollen and tender. Signs of pneumonia had also developed. Salicin was given freely, and in forty-eight hours the articular symptoms subsided. The next day the temperature came down rapidly, and there was considerable collapse, which passed off, and the boy got quickly well. The heart remained unaffected.

The second case is that of a boy now under my care at St. Mary's.[1] He was admitted with signs of some consolidation and pleuritic effusion on the left

F. G. H——, Albert ward, December 1888.

side, and cough. Three days later both wrists and knees became stiff, tender, and swollen; the temperature was 103°. Under salicin the arthritis quickly subsided, and the boy made a quick and rapid recovery.

It may be that in such cases the pleurisy is simply the direct result of chill, just as the articular rheumatism is the result of chill, both being due to a common cause. Yet, pleurisy comes sufficiently often later still in the course of acute articular rheumatism, when it can hardly be attributed to the initial chill, and when there is no serious cardiac change to account for its origin in mechanical congestion, to render its immediate dependence upon the rheumatic virus highly probable.

## LECTURE III.

Pericarditis—Its connection with other phases of rheumatism—
Special characteristics in childhood—Subacute, recurrent, dry—
Tendency to fibrosis and chronic thickening rather than to effusion
—Endocarditis; subacute and recurrent likewise—Special liability of children and of young girls—Connection of endocarditis with other phases of rheumatism—The endocarditis of chorea—
Relation of pericarditis and endocarditis to the evolution of nodules—Morbid changes in nodules and cardiac valves analogous—Significance of this—Different forms of valvular disease
—Mitral stenosis—Early signs—Double second sound at the apex
—Hypertrophy and dilatation—Comparative rarity of dropsy—
The mode of death differs from that met with in adults—Scarlatinal rheumatism—Rheumatoid arthritis—Special points in treatment.

PERICARDITIS is admitted into the rheumatic series without question. It is, I think, undisputed that inflammation of the pericardium owns rheumatism as its most common cause. Pericarditis may appear at any point in the rheumatic procession of events—first or last, alone or in combination with other phases. Most often it comes late, after endocarditis, especially when the heart is already hypertrophied and dilated. Sometimes it is associated with the valvular inflammation, is often accompanied by the evolution of nodules, and not unfrequently arises in connection with chorea. The development of pericarditis in association with chorea apart from articular rheumatism is a link of association between them which is of considerable significance. Examples of different combinations and the place of pericarditis are shown in the illustrative cases, especially in Series II., VI., and X., and in the case of Kate B—— given in the first lecture, as well as in some examples which I am about to put before you. But the pericarditis with which we are most familiar—the acute general pericarditis of rheumatic fever—is not representative of the disease in children. The extreme distress; the panting, shallow respiration; the fluttering, irregular pulse; the strange delirium; the physical signs of friction all over the cardiac area as lymph is poured out; the extensive dulness, often following quickly as serous effusion takes place, spreading high up to the second or third rib; the muffled heart's sounds; the raised apex—all these classical signs are sometimes wanting, at other times largely modified, in the rheumatic pericarditis of childhood in its most usual form.

Such cases of acute general pericarditis do occur in the acute rheumatism of childhood, as well as in

## THE ACUTE FORM

adults, but they form the exception. I have just had under my care at St. Mary's a girl of seven, Elizabeth S——,[1] who developed most acute pericarditis with chorea, and died of it in ten days. There was not the slightest accompanying articular affection, not the smallest joint pain or tenderness; the temperature ranged between 98° and 100° only except for one night, when it reached 101·5°; but—most evil sign— the pulse ran up to 130 and 140. The child had had slight articular rheumatism seven months previously, and again a fortnight before admission and prior to the chorea. Her father had had rheumatic fever; her sister aged twelve, subacute rheumatism. There was a rumbling mitral murmur. The child was thin, pallid, and feeble. The progress of anæmia since the advent of pericarditis was most remarkable; in the last few days of life it became extreme. Moreover—what I will ask you to mark especially—there were no nodules, so common an accompaniment of cardiac inflammation in a child, whether it be endocardial or pericardial, as I pointed out before. This very acute inflammation appears to be less identified with the development of nodules than the more chronic form.

Let me give another example of intensely acute

[1] Children's ward, December 1888.

general pericarditis, associated with equally extreme chorea, probably rheumatic. M. B——, a girl of fifteen, was admitted under my care at St. Mary's Hospital in August, 1885, with chorea of the most violent kind, rapid respiration and panting dyspnœa. She had been ill about three weeks, but it was impossible to obtain any clear history, for the people who brought the patient could give us little information about her, and the girl herself was unable to utter a word. She made frantic attempts to speak, but could not articulate, uttering only unintelligible sounds. The jactitations were so violent that she had to be fastened down in bed, and it was not possible to examine the chest satisfactorily, so constant and uncontrollable were the movements. By the aid of two nurses I was just able to make out that the area of cardiac dulness was increased, the heart's sounds—as, indeed, extreme feebleness of the pulse showed—were almost inaudible, and a faint friction-sound could be detected at one point. The diagnosis was rheumatic chorea and pericarditis with some effusion. Before evening, a few hours after admission, the patient died. On post-mortem examination, extensive pericarditis was found, the pericardial sac being greatly distended with turbid, flaky, sero-purulent fluid, and the surfaces thinly coated with recent lymph. There was also inflammatory thickening of the mitral valve. In this instance, the chorea, endocarditis, and pericarditis occurring in the same individual stamped the case as almost certainly rheumatic.

Now, instances of extremely acute pericardial inflammation like these occur as they do in adults. But this is not the most frequent and typical form of pericarditis in children. It usually occurs insidiously; a slight pericardial rub is noted perhaps, which may cease or continue without much change; the child is seen to be restless and uncomfortable, and complains of pain in the præcordial region; the pulse quickens to 120 or 130; the anæmia increases to a marked degree; the chorea, if present, becomes a little aggravated perhaps, or curious emotional attacks come on, the child being moved to tears or laughter by a word; the temperature is slightly raised, perhaps to 100° or 101°, but often remains normal if there is no accompanying arthritis, or pleurisy, or pneumonia; and with this a mitral murmur develops, or an existing one grows rougher, and subcutaneous nodules begin to appear on the elbows and knees, or ankles or occiput. The pericardial rub continues, or subsides after a few days, to reappear again after an interval perhaps, or, although it never reappears, the rapid action of the heart continues, in spite of digitalis, or belladonna, or strophanthus, or ergot; fresh nodules come out; the area of cardiac dulness increases, and there is muffling of the sounds over the mid-cardiac region, but no sign of effusion; the heart is clearly growing more bulky and the pericardium thicker, and emaciation and anæmia proceed apace. The child daily grows more pallid, weak, and wasted; the pulse grows more feeble; and so, without extreme dyspnœa or dropsy, the patient sinks slowly from exhaustion and heart-failure.

Such, gentlemen, is a picture of the pericarditis of childhood in its most usual form, so frequently associated with the evolution of subcutaneous nodules, often with endocarditis, and often with chorea. It represents very closely the case of J. T——, Series X. And mark what is found after death: usually the two surfaces of the pericardium glued together by a thick layer of adhesive lymph; the pericardium itself greatly thickened; the walls of the sac tough, dense, fibrous tissue, an eighth of an inch thick, perhaps; the chronic inflammatory process spreading sometimes from the external sac to the anterior mediastinum, so that these are matted together in a thick fibrous mass—' indurative mediastino-pericarditis,' as seen in the specimen from one of these cases now before you.

Take, again, the case of C. H. B—— (Series II.), a boy of six, who was admitted to the Hospital for Sick Children on May 8, 1888. The boy had never complained of anything until five weeks before, when he had stiffness in that typical place which I mentioned in the first lecture—viz. the hamstring tendons—and in the ankles; but they were not noticed to be swollen or tender. Then he had pains in the shoulders, and then in the chest, for which he was poulticed; but he was never kept in bed, nor was it thought necessary for a doctor to see him, although he was observed to be very breathless on exertion. The pains were supposed to be growing pains merely; rheumatism was not thought of. Latterly he had grown very excitable and nervous, and had twitching of the limbs. On examination, he was found to have a double mitral murmur with a highly accentuated second sound, and considerable hypertrophy; the dulness reached to the left edge of the sternum, and upwards as high as the third rib; the apex-beat was in the fifth space, three-quarters of an inch outside the left nipple—so that the valve disease must have been of considerable standing, due to endocarditis of much earlier date than the late articular pains. There was also discovered a crop of fibrous nodules on the elbows, knees, and malleoli, so small as not to attract attention unless carefully looked for. The boy was extremely anæmic; the pulse suspiciously rapid (124). By the end of the month these nodules had attained considerable size, and on June 9th a fresh development of still larger nodules took place on the back of the head, the malleoli, and the knees; with this, pericardial friction occurred two days later, and great pain in the cardiac region, relieved by poultice. In a week's time all pericardial friction had disappeared, but the boy remained pale and anxious, the pulse was quick and irregular, pleuritic friction was heard at the base of both lungs, and the systolic mitral bruit had become musical. A month later (July 14th) a third crop of nodules of large size appeared on the knees and elbows. The cardiac excitement continued, the pulse ranging from 130 to 140; pain in the chest came on; emaciation and anæmia were progressive. No friction could be heard, but the increasing area of cardiac dulness, the rapidity of pulse, which neither digitalis nor any other drug could control, showed no diminution; and thus, in spite of all treatment, the boy went from bad to worse, and died from heart-failure on September 6, just four months after admission. It is to be noted how in this case the grave symptoms proceeded *pari passu* with the eruption of large nodules, rapid pulse, progressive anæmia and emaciation, and how steadily and resistlessly the disease marched on in this way to a fatal end, uncontrolled by any remedial agent.

Take again another case, that of Arthur C——, a boy of eleven, who is now under my care at Great Ormond Street Hospital. He came into hospital first in September 1888, with subacute arthritis, great anæmia, a loud double mitral murmur, and great hypertrophy. He quickly went out convalescent, but was brought back on November 12th, again failing in health. On the 22nd the temperature, which had been normal, rose to 101, and well-marked double tonsillitis followed. This was over in three days, and the temperature fell to normal; but a week later (November 28) he became restless, his respirations went up to 32 and his pulse to 112, he had headache, and vomited. The following day (the 29th) the first sign of nodules was detected on the knees and elbows. The heart's action became more excited; by December 6 it was violent, and the anæmia had greatly increased; the nodules had grown larger, some to the size of small peas, and a pericardial friction-sound was audible. The temperature has fallen since to normal, but the pulse keeps between 100 and 112, and there has been dyspnœa at times. The friction continues, the anæmia increases, and the prognosis is most grave. Note here, again, the rapid pulse, the increasing anæmia, and the development of nodules concurrently with the development of progressive intractable pericarditis.[1]

Rheumatic pericarditis, then, in early life is apt to be subacute, persistent, recurrent, and progressive; going on, not for days only, but for weeks or months; the inflamed membrane slowly or intermittently exuding, not serum, but adhesive lymph, causing adhesions more or less complete, and development of fibrous tissue, so that the pericardium becomes thickened, sometimes enormously, as you see in the specimen produced. This form of subacute progressive pericarditis might almost be called 'nodular,' so frequent is the evolution of these significant bodies associated with it. Their eruption appears to have a deep meaning; when they are numerous and large, they indicate a condition so grave, and apparently often so uncontrollable, that, as I said before,

[1] This unfavourable prognosis has since been verified. The pericarditis continued in spite of treatment, anæmia and dyspnœa increased, and the boy died about six weeks later. Post-mortem examination revealed general dry pericarditis, with great thickening, and nearly complete adhesion.

I have come to regard them as almost a sentence of death.

What is the pathological relation of the fibrous nodule to the fibrosis of the pericardium? It would seem as if the same virus or influence which stirs up the inflammatory change in the fibrous tissues of sheaths and tendons, and which results in the formation of nodules, stirs up in the same way fibrous organisation of lymph or proliferation of the fibrous tissue of the pericardium. Dr. Barlow found in one case that the pericardial adhesions had a distinctly nodular character;[1] and Dr. Angel Money,[2] in a similar case, with extreme pericardial adhesion, found a distinct nodule extending from the pericardium inwards, and invading the heart's substance. I believe that the fatal issue is largely dependent upon the tightening grip of the adherent contracting thickened pericardium, strangling, as it were, the muscle and muscular movements of an often already crippled heart; possibly also the heart-muscle is weakened by fibrous interstitial invasion and by concurrent myocarditis; hence the rapid pulse and the progressive feebleness of cardiac action. The effect of the continued constriction of the heart by the tough, thickened pericardial casing in early life

[1] *Brit. Med. Jour.* September 15, 1883, p. 511.   [2] *Ibid.*

upon the due growth of the heart itself was first brought home to my mind some years ago by the following remarkable case.

A girl, aged nineteen, was admitted into St. Mary's Hospital with general dropsy, for which no satisfactory cause could be made out. She had no signs of either cardiac or renal disease, but she had considerable ascites and hydrothorax, for which she was repeatedly tapped. At last she died. On postmortem examination, the heart was found tightly enclosed in a bag of dense unyielding fibrous tissue, the adherent pericardium enormously thickened; the heart itself was as small as that of a child of ten years old; there was no other lesion of any kind. There could be no doubt that the girl had had fibrous pericarditis as a child, and the embarrassed heart, tightly embraced by the contracting tissue, could not grow; at length, becoming unequal to carry on the circulation of the enlarging vascular system, dropsy followed. Sir T. Watson[1] observed a similar result. He says: 'When the adhesion takes place during youth, as in connection with acute rheumatism it is very apt to do, it seems to prevent the further growth of the heart, and virtually leads to atrophy of that organ or a disproportionate smallness of its

[1] *Principles and Practice of Physic*, 4th ed. vol. ii. p. 301.

cavities, vessels, and general size'; and Bouillaud mentions the case of a woman, aged sixty-one, whose heart was the size of that of a child's of ten or twelve, and marked by furrows and opaque spots from old pericarditis.[1] Usually, however, in the case of children, the pericarditis persists or recurs, or it comes late, when the heart is already dilated and hypertrophied from valvular disease, and the new clog, the tightening grip of the pericardium, is more deadly than it would be to the normal organ. The heart is not small, but enlarged, and although one may believe that its further development might be interfered with, yet death usually takes place before the disproportion between heart-growth and the development of the rest of the body has become conspicuous or extreme.

*Endocarditis.*—Endocarditis occurs acutely in the course of articular rheumatism in children, just as it does in adults. The position of endocarditis as one of the rheumatic inflammations is like that of pericarditis, established and allowed. Yet in childhood it often occurs quite apart from any concurrent affection of the joints; and it may develop at any period in the rheumatic procession of events, early

[1] Payne's, Jones', and Sieveking's *Pathological Anatomy*, 2nd ed. p. 344.

or late, in combination with arthritis or pericarditis, or chorea, or nodules, with any or all of these combined. Usually it comes early in the series, and recurs later, in contrast to pericarditis, which is more apt to appear towards the end. An example of this is given in Series II., where it came first. The rule is : endocarditis early ; pericarditis late. But as with pericarditis, so with endocarditis ; the acute form in connection with severe articular rheumatism is far less common than one slight and trivial apparently at the time, accompanying an equally slight articular affection or chorea ; all sign of it perhaps disappearing for a season, yet recurring and persisting until the injury to the valve becomes serious and finally fatal. It is not, as it is so commonly with adults, a sharp attack of endocarditis accompanying the articular affection, ceasing with it, and followed slowly by chronic after-changes in the valve or muscle ; but subacute, insidious, progressive.

In the first lecture I endeavoured to show how an extremely slight and transient arthritis, hardly noticeable, not recognised as rheumatic, probably not coming under a doctor's observation at all, might be accompanied by valvulitis, running on unsuspected at the time, and only discovered afterwards when great cardiac changes have developed. Dr. Sibson, whose name will always be honoured in this Society, affirmed that the more severe the rheumatic attack, the greater the tendency to cardiac inflammation. Probably this is so. Severe attacks of articular rheumatism are, however, rare in young children; and, light as the arthritis usually is, children are nearly twice as liable to cardiac inflammation as adults.[1]

Valvular disease of the heart in childhood is not invariably the result of rheumatic endocarditis. There are certain exceptions. We may exclude the cases of congenital disease and those where the endocarditis is set up by one of the specific fevers, or the septic or uræmic poison. There will remain for consideration three classes—viz. (1) those cases in which the valvular affection arises in association with distinct attacks of articular rheumatism; (2) those associated with chorea in which no articular affection is observed; and (3) those in which no connection with any other morbid condition of any kind can be traced—what may be called the 'unexplained cases.'

Now, with regard to the first class, cases of heart affection connected with articular rheumatism, the organic change would, I think, be generally allowed to be due to rheumatic endocarditis. And these

---

[1] *Collective Investigation Record*, vol. iv. p. 71.

form the largest proportion. Dr. West[1] gives statistics of 135 cases of organic valvular disease, of which in 60 per cent. rheumatism was 'either known or asserted on good grounds to have been the starting point of the mischief'; and he quotes the estimate of M. Roger as 78 per cent., and that of M. Cadet de Gassicourt as 81 per cent. Dr. Goodhart's statistics yield 62 per cent.[2] My own statistics of 195 cases specially examined and investigated for the purpose, including the evidence of rheumatic fever in parents or immediate blood-relatives, give 79 per cent.[3] All these are based upon the occurrence of articular rheumatism only, and the absence of evidence of this in any given case is not to be taken as positive proof of its non-rheumatic nature.

The only question which arises, then, is with regard to the two remaining groups, those associated with chorea alone, and the group of unexplained cases. Are these the result of rheumatic endocarditis? Taking the latter first, their number is not large. Dr. Goodhart, out of 248 cases of heart-disease, found all but 55 associated with either rheumatism or chorea.[4] If from this remainder we take the con-

[1] *Diseases of Infancy and Childhood*, 7th ed., p. 553.
[2] *Diseases of Children*, pp. 528-9.
[3] *Lancet*, October 31, 1885, p. 795.
[4] *Diseases of Children*, p. 529.

genital, pyæmic, and fever cases there are few left unexplained, and of these few many are probably rheumatic, where slight arthritis has been overlooked or been absent. There remain, then, practically only the choreic cases—i.e. the cases where organic heart-disease arises in chorea, but is not known to be associated with any manifestation of articular rheumatism. Are these to be included as examples of rheumatic endocarditis? In my judgment most of them—possibly all. The antecedent probability is largely in favour of their rheumatic origin. My reasons are these. The cardiac affection of chorea is, as a rule, organic, not merely functional. Functional murmurs do no doubt arise occasionally in chorea—e.g. the ordinary hæmic murmur of the pulmonary orifice. But that the mitral murmur of chorea is not usually of functional origin seems to be established by the following considerations:—

1. If the mitral murmur were what is called hæmic, it is strange that in this particular disease—chorea alone—the mitral valve should be the seat of it, such functional disturbance being in other conditions associated with the pulmonary and aortic orifices; and further, if a mitral hæmic murmur did exist, à *fortiori* a pulmonary one should exist also, but it does not. Moreover, the mitral murmur of

chorea comes early as a rule, before anæmia and debility arise.

2. The hypothesis that the mitral murmur of chorea is commonly spasmodic or paretic as suggested by Dr. Sturges, although plausible and ingenious, is a pure hypothesis, unsupported by positive evidence. It is rendered improbable by the fact that, as a matter of clinical observation, the murmur does not arise especially in connection with irregular action of the heart, as I have repeatedly satisfied myself; and, moreover, as Dr. Osler [1] points out, the general immunity of involuntary muscle in all choreic disturbance is against the theory of spasm; while, as to paresis, the murmurs have no special association with paretic chorea.

3. In fatal cases of chorea endocarditis is almost invariably found *post mortem*. There is no other disease in which it is so constant.[2]

4. In fatal cases of valvular disease arising in association with chorea, the changes found in the valves *post mortem* are identical with those from endocarditis from other causes, while the valve chiefly affected is the mitral valve, the one most liable to endocarditis.

[1] *American Journal of Medical Sciences*, vol. xciv. new series, p. 374.
[2] *Ibid.* p. 375.

These considerations are borne out by careful clinical observations, such as those of Dr. Stephen Mackenzie and Dr. Osler. The former found the murmur of chorea persistent in 60 to 80 per cent. from one to five years afterwards.[1] Dr. Osler, independently pursuing a similar inquiry, comes to a like result. In 110 cases of chorea examined two years afterwards, organic heart-disease was found in 54.[2] A large proportion of choreic murmurs therefore persist or reappear, and in some instances do not develop until after the chorea, when all motor and paretic disturbance has long ceased.

The valvular affection of the heart, then, in chorea is, in the vast majority of cases, organic, due to endocarditis. Is the endocarditis rheumatic? The evidence in favour of this is extremely strong. First, there is the frequent association of articular rheumatism with chorea and endocarditis together; secondly, the frequent association of articular rheumatism with the two independently, with chorea on the one hand, and with endocarditis on the other; thirdly, the especial association of endocarditis with those cases of chorea which are also associated with articular rheumatism. The great proportion of cases

[1] *Trans. Int. Med. Cong.* 1881, vol. iv. pp. 100, 104.
[2] *American Journal of Medical Sciences*, vol. xciv. new series.

of endocarditis which arise in connection with chorea arise in choreas connected with articular rheumatism. Endocarditis picks out, so to speak, the rheumatic cases. In 84 cases of chorea of which I took precise notes there was a history of articular rheumatism in either the patient or near blood-relatives in 62. In the remaining 22 there was no such history. Of the 62 cases of chorea with rheumatic history, 43, or 69 per cent., had organic heart-disease. In the 22 choreas without rheumatic history there were only 6 cases of organic heart-disease, or 27 per cent.[1] The statistics of the Collective Investigation Committee tell the same story. They yield 50 per cent. of heart affection in choreas with rheumatic history, as against 35 per cent. in those without rheumatic history; and these statistics, as stated, necessarily give too low an estimate of the rheumatic influence, since the only test of rheumatism admitted is the antecedent or concurrent association of articular affection. Yet the evidence afforded by nodules, by pericarditis, and by erythema exudativum is of considerable weight. How suggestive, for example, are cases of chorea such as that of the child I exhibited at the last lecture, who has a plentiful crop of nodules accompanying endocar-

[1] *Lancet*, October 31, 1885, p. 794.

ditis, yet in whom there is no history of articular affection at any time, either in the patient or her family;[1] and that of the girl now under my care at St. Mary's Hospital,[2] who came in with chorea, and has since developed pericarditis, with only the slightest and most transient articular affection, lasting no longer than twenty-four hours. Lastly, there is the indirect evidence afforded by the significant fact to which I drew attention in the last lecture—namely, the singular harmony which exists between the incidence of articular rheumatism, of chorea, of rheumatic chorea, and of choreic heart-disease, upon the sexes between the ages of eleven and fifteen. If the statistics are to be trusted, girls are from two to three times as liable as boys to articular rheumatism, to chorea, to rheumatic chorea, to heart-disease in rheumatic chorea, and to heart-disease in chorea where there is no history of rheumatism. And apart from all direct evidence of rheu-

[1] Sarah M——, admitted to the Hospital for Sick Children, November 15, 1888, under Dr. Barlow. Since the above was written a very significant series of events has occurred—namely, acute tonsillitis, followed after an interval of a fortnight by pain, swelling, and tenderness of one small joint only, that of the right middle finger; this lasted two days, and then disappeared. On the same day pericardial friction was discovered, and still continued when this note was taken a week later.
[2] Kate B——, Albert Victor ward, January 1889.

matism, when endocarditis appears in association with chorea, in view of the fact that rheumatism is the chief cause of endocarditis on the one hand, and that it is the only disease closely associated with chorea on the other, is it not more reasonable to suppose, when endocarditis and chorea occur together, that rheumatism is at the root of both, rather than that the valvular inflammation is set up by disordered muscular action, or that it depends upon some mysterious condition connected with chorea of which we know nothing?

It has been suggested that strain, or shock, or violent action of the valves is the source of choreic endocarditis. This is, I think, untenable, for many good reasons. In the first place, the heart does *not* act violently in chorea, but feebly; tension is lessened, not increased. Secondly, in diseases such as exophthalmic goître, where the valves flap to with great force, valvulitis is not thereby set up, although a functional murmur is sometimes developed. Thirdly, heart-disease does not arise especially in connection with chorea associated with fright, when a sudden strain might be postulated, but in connection with chorea associated with rheumatism equally whether fright is or is not present as a co-factor. The most cogent argument of all, however, is that drawn from pericarditis. Pericarditis arises in chorea quite apart from any articular affection as often in proportion to its general frequency as endocarditis. How is this to be accounted for? Neither the strain hypothesis, the paretic hypothesis, nor the spasm hypothesis will explain choreic pericarditis any more than it will explain choreic nodules or choreic erythema. So far the only reasonable explanation of the endocarditis of chorea, as of the pericarditis, is that it is of rheumatic origin. As Dr. Barlow has surmised, and as I shall endeavour to demonstrate presently, the active morbid change in the cardiac valves in subacute endocarditis appears to be analogous to that in the subcutaneous fibrous tissues giving rise to nodules. Such nodules are frequently developed without concurrent articular rheumatism, but with endocarditis, in the course of chorea. Is it not probable that in choreic endocarditis a subacute change of this kind goes on, and that many of the murmurs at least which come and go or develop afterwards are really due to this cause, rather than to functional disorder? The endocardial change may be sometimes just as passing or recurrent as we have seen the nodular development to be in many cases.

Turning now from the evidence that the endocarditis of childhood is chiefly rheumatic to the consideration of the condition in itself, I have said that it is less acute, severe, and passing than with adults; that it is especially liable to relapse, and recur, or smoulder on for weeks or months. This is well shown in the case of W. S—— (Series VIII.), where endocarditis, beginning in 1886, occurred again in 1887, and then continued with arthritis, chorea, erythema, and nodules, pretty constantly, until the rheumatic series closed in death in March, 1888. The cases of H. W. B—— (Series I.), C. H. B—— (Series II.), and J. T—— (Series X.) afford additional illustrations.

In the case of B. H——, a boy aged six years and a-half, now under my care in Great Ormond Street Hospital, a similar slow recurrent endocarditis is going on. The boy has never had any sign of what is ordinarily termed rheumatism, except some pains in the feet attributed to an accident, with pain in the cardiac region and sweating; but there is a history of rheumatism on the mother's side. He has a well-marked mitral regurgitant murmur and reduplicated second sound at the apex. Nodules are being developed; he grows more pale and ill; has had two attacks of sudden dyspnœa, with signs of circumscribed pneumonia, evidently embolic. Fresh nodules continue to appear; the murmur grows harsher and more musical. There can be little doubt that chronic endocarditis is going on, and that the injury to the heart-structures is progressive.

A more striking instance still is that of H. G——, a boy aged fourteen, whose case I have published before,[1] and which I shall therefore allude to only very briefly here. The patient had large nodules on the flexor tendons of the palms and fingers, accompanied by subacute recurrent endocarditis, which had probably commenced with an attack of slight arthritis about a year previously. The joint rheumatism had received no serious attention; the heart was not examined. The boy continued to follow athletic sports, with the result of setting up extreme regurgitant aortic disease and dilatation of the left ventricle. It is interesting to note, in passing, that the boy's sister had had chorea without any articular rheumatism; his grandmother, rheumatic fever.

The eruption of subcutaneous nodules is associated with grave progressive endocarditis as closely as with progressive pericarditis; and I think an examination of the pathological process going on in the valves in

[1] Lectures on Heart-Disease in Children (*Lancet*, October 17, 1885, p. 703).

# 104 RHEUMATIC INFLAMMATION OF MITRAL VALVE

Fig. 1.

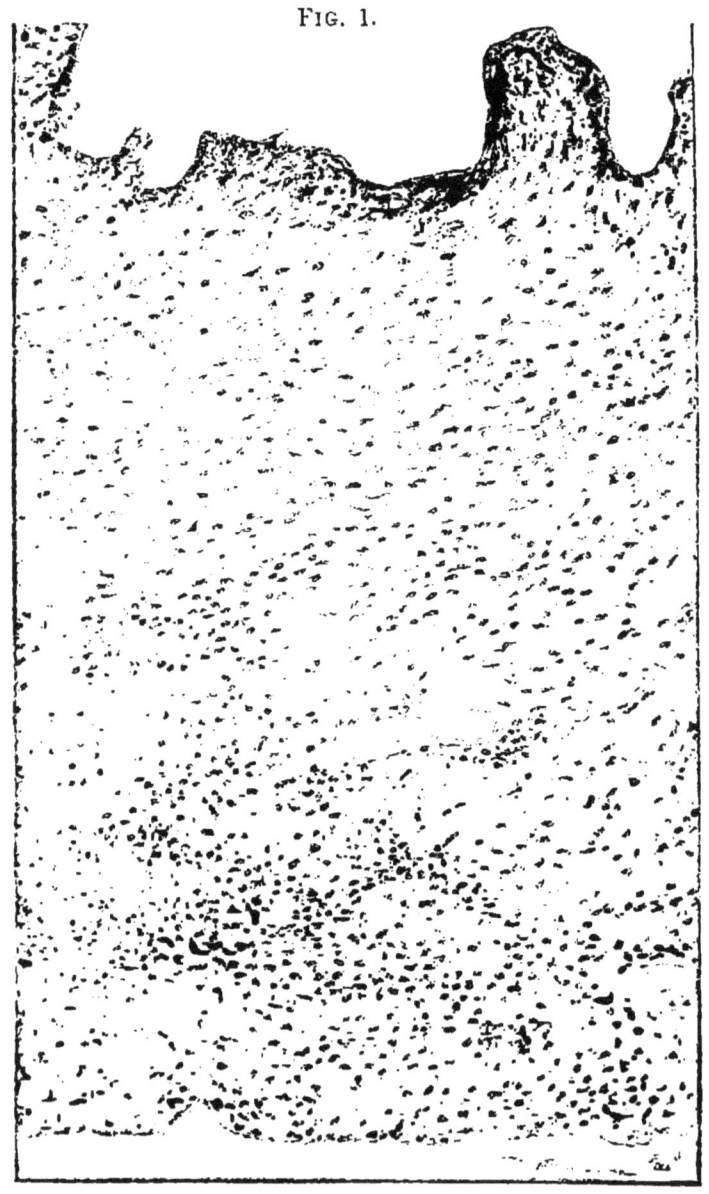

Microscopic appearances in a section of the mitral valve in a case of rheumatic endocarditis in a child, showing proliferation and cell-infiltration of subendothelial fibrous tissue. (Ellen M——, aged eight years and a-half; Hospital for Sick Children, Great Ormond Street; Dr. Barlow; March 28, 1883. Arthritis, nodules, morbus cordis, purpura.)

FIG. 2.

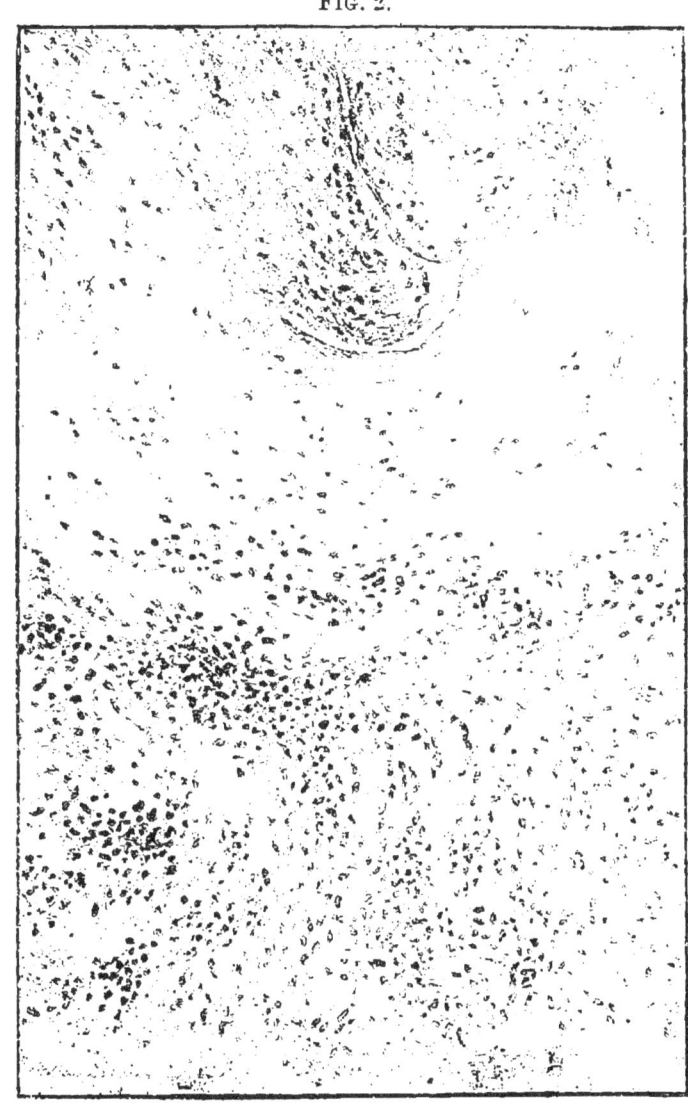

Microscopic appearances in a section of subcutaneous tendinous nodule in acute rheumatism, showing active proliferation and cell-infiltration of fibrous tissue. (John T——, aged seven years and a-half; Hospital for Sick Children, Great Ormond Street; died August 6, 1888. Chorea, arthritis, endocarditis, pleurisy, nodules, pericarditis.)

endocarditis of this kind explains the connection. The inflammatory process in the valves, as Dr. Barlow ventured to anticipate seven years ago, appears to be identical with that met with in the nodules—viz. nuclear proliferation, cell infiltration, spindle cells in process of transformation into fibrous tissue, wavy bands of fibres, and vessels. The microscopic appearances of a thin section of the mitral valve of the patient, Ellen M——, are shown in the specimens exhibited, for which I am indebted to Mr. Priestley, and reproduced in the drawing (Fig. 1), and those in a subcutaneous nodule in Fig. 2. The proliferation and cell infiltration of the fibrous tissue which forms the framework of the valve is the most conspicuous feature, and it is to the proliferation of this layer that most of the swelling is due. There is, moreover, infiltration of the whole thickness of the valve with round cells, nuclei, or leucocytes. In some specimens there can be seen distinct proliferation of the endothelium, and in some a deposit of fibrin on the surface in which leucocytes are visible. But the chief change—the greatest and most important change, that which causes the thickening and rigidity—is the proliferation of fibrous tissue, which is the leading feature of the morbid process seen in the subcutaneous nodule. Now, looking at the affection of the fibrous tissues of the joints of the subcutaneous fascia, of tendons, of the pericardium, and of the endocardium, it appears that the *materies morbi* of rheumatism, whatever its nature, sets up similar irritant changes in fibrous tissues in all these parts. But since the nodules are rarely found in adults, although so common in children, and that endocarditis and pericarditis are likewise more common in children, while arthritis, on the other hand, is less severe, it would appear further, that in early life the fibrous tissues of subcutaneous fasciæ, of tendons, of pericardium, and of endocardium are far more sensitive to the morbid stimulus, more easily excited to proliferation, than the same tissues in later life; while, on the contrary, the joint fibrous tissues are less susceptible to the poison in children than in adults. It seems clear, moreover, that the susceptibility of subcutaneous fibrous tissues and the susceptibility of the fibrous tissues of endocardium and pericardium go together; and this circumstance, as suggested before, affords a possible clue to the nature of the evanescent mitral murmurs of rheumatic arthritis and chorea. The rapid development of the nodules in some instances in the course of a few days even, and their equally quick disappearance on occasion, suggest that the murmur which arises and disappears, and which is styled functional, is really caused by the development of similar inflammatory cell-growth in the valves and chordæ, which may subside in them as quickly as we see it does in a subcutaneous nodule. This correlation of nodules and valvulitis gives the appearance of the former great clinical significance, as probably indicative of a similar change going on in endocardium or pericardium, or both. When the nodules are few or small, they must be regarded as serious signs; when large and numerous, they are grave warnings of the existence of a condition of ultimate danger.

Ulcerative endocarditis is most rare in the rheumatism of children, since it is met with chiefly in patients broken down by drink and disease. The earliest age at which I find its occurrence recorded is in a patient of my own at the Children's Hospital, Annie I——, a girl of eight.[1] Senator observed it in a boy of fourteen, and Dr. Ord in a girl of sixteen. It possesses no special features which require notice here.

Rheumatic endocarditis in children, as in adults, attacks mitral, aortic, and tricuspid valves, the former by far the most commonly; mitral regurgitation

[1] *Post-mortem Book*, vol. iv. 1887.

is the most usual resulting lesion, although mitral stenosis is far more frequent than is generally supposed. It is in the latter that the chief interest centres.

It is well known that mitral stenosis is met with most frequently in young women. Of 263 cases collected by Sir Dyce Duckworth,[1] there were 177 females and 86 males. And this relation between the sexes probably holds good in the case of children, in accordance with the great preponderance of heart disease in girls between eleven and fifteen. Mitral stenosis is in its origin especially a lesion of childhood and early life. I find 33 cases with presystolic murmur and 24 with reduplicated second sound at the apex, indicating commencing stenosis, out of 273 cases of organic heart-disease in children of which I have accurate record. The youngest patients were two boys of four. Yet the age of the youngest patient in Sir Dyce Duckworth's list was fourteen. Dr. Fagge had no instance under ten;[2] Dr. Hayden two only of seven years old.[3]

It was formerly taught that mitral stenosis is less often rheumatic than any other valvular affection. As a matter of actual fact, this form of heart-disease

[1] *Etiology of Mitral Stenosis* (pamphlet).
[2] *Guy's Hospital Reports*, Series 3, vol. xii.
[3] *Diseases of the Heart* (Dublin, 1875), p. 964 *et seq.*

—in children at any rate—is especially rheumatic, and because it is so associated with the rheumatic endocarditis of childhood I lay stress upon it here. Dr. Sansom found 50 per cent. with a history of articular rheumatism or of pains.[1] Sir Dyce Duckworth's cases yield 60 per cent. My own statistics are still more remarkable. Taking children alone, I find this striking evidence of its rheumatic relation. Of 57 cases, in 44 there was acute rheumatism in the patient; in 20 of these 44 in the family also; in 4 more in the family alone, leaving 9 only in which there was no rheumatic history. Putting out of the question family history, then, there was personal history of rheumatism in 44 out of 57, or 79 per cent.

It is in the period of childhood that mitral stenosis most commonly commences. The reason why it has not been more frequently observed is perhaps due to the fact that it is at this period usually in the initial stage. It is, as Dr. Sansom has shown,[2] the special product of the slight, subacute, slow, recurrent, rheumatic endocarditis which is characteristic of childhood. The stenosis does not generally reach the degree when it is proclaimed by the loud, vibrating, prolonged presystolic murmur,

---

[1] *Lettsomian Lectures*, 2nd ed. p. 130.
[2] *Ibid.* 1886, p. 80.

until a few years have passed. The slight rumble, or the reduplicated second sound, escapes notice, or attention is drawn away from it by an accompanying regurgitant bruit. Hence it is discovered later, with startling frequency, just after childhood. Cases are met with in which this condition is found to exist without any rheumatic attack to explain it. In these instances I believe it has had its first origin in childhood, arising unnoticed with a slight arthritis, or a crop of nodules, or a chorea, or alone, as the sole manifestation of a rheumatic outburst.

The earliest sign of mitral stenosis is reduplication of the second sound *at the apex*. Dr. Sansom has observed generally,[1] that 'reduplication of the first or of the second sound is an early sign of stenosis.' But I would limit the statement to reduplication at the apex, audible over the mitral area only, or at least having its maximum intensity there. Dr. Sansom gives two cases[2] in which this local limitation was observed, but he does not differentiate them from the rest. Now, although reduplication of both first and second sounds, audible over the aortic and pulmonary valves at the base of the heart, occurs in certain cases of mitral stenosis, it is not this with

---

[1] *Lettsomian Lectures*, p. 22.
[2] *Trans. Med. Soc.* vol. v. p. 204.

which I am concerned; that is not an early sign according to my experience. It is reduplication *at the apex* which is the significant early sign; basic reduplication usually comes later, with a pronounced presystolic murmur or with mitral regurgitation, and it is explained readily enough by the difference in tension in the pulmonary artery and aorta, causing asynchronous closure of their respective valves. It appears, however, to be generally assumed that this asynchronism of the pulmonary and aortic valves will account for *all* reduplication. But it certainly entirely fails to explain reduplications audible only at the apex. If the doubling of the sound were caused by the asynchronous closure of the aortic and pulmonary valves, it would be audible over their position—i.e. at the base of the heart,—but it is not. Dr. Sansom saw this difficulty and to him the credit of a more correct explanation is due. He suggests that the *first* of the two second sounds is the normal one caused by the simultaneous closure of the pulmonary and aortic valves, and the *second* by the sudden tension of the mitral flaps as the ventricle relaxes. The blood in the auricle, in a state of increased tension, drives open the mitral door, and, rushing round the sides of the ventricle, gets underneath the curtains—the anterior one of which, as Dr. Macalister has shown, is stretched tight from the basal ring to the top of the papillary muscle—and thus gives rise to a sound of tension.[1] This explanation is, I think, correct in the main—so far as this, at least: that one of the two second sounds—viz. the second—is mitral in origin. It is not audible at the base; only one sound is audible over the aortic and pulmonary area, while two are audible over the mitral area. The one which is heard over the mitral only must be produced there. It seems to me that the most probable explanation is that the *first* of the two second sounds is the normal one caused by the click of the basic valves, as Dr. Sansom suggests, the pulmonary element being accentuated and rendered louder by increased resistance in front. The *second* of the two second sounds is due to the smack or click of the forcible opening of the swollen, rigid mitral with shortened chords, kept closed with difficulty by the contracting ventricle, and springing back suddenly as the ventricle relaxes and exerts its suction power, aided by the increased tension in the left auricle, rather than by the auricular contraction, which occurs later. The suction power of the relaxing ventricle has been shown by Marcy and Fick, and Goltz and Gubler, to be considerable at the beginning of dia-

[1] *Lettsomian Lectures*, 2nd ed. p. 123.

stole, possibly as much as 23 millimetres of mercury, independent of respiration.[1] This view is supported by the fact that, after the *second* of the two second sounds—i.e. the one which Dr. Sansom and myself take to be the *mitral* sound—there is in some instances a soft bruit, a distinct diastolic murmur, probably due to the rush of blood through the narrowed aperture caused by the auricular contraction which comes, not at the very beginning of diastole, but a moment after its commencement. Reduplication of the second sound at the apex, then, is, I think, the earliest sign of swelling and rigidity of the mitral flaps, and consequent imperfect opening of the valve. Whether the explanation I have given be accepted or not, there can be no question as to the connection of this morbid sound with early mitral stenosis, and of its clinical significance.

*Hypertrophy and Dilatation.*— These secondary changes proceed more rapidly in children than in adults. The first develops apace, in accordance with the general law before mentioned—that the tissues respond to stimulation and grow more rapidly in childhood; and the second—dilatation—perhaps because the tissues are more soft and yielding.

The following is an example of rapid dilatation

[1] Macalister: *Brit. Med. Jour.* October 28, 1882, p. 123.

and hypertrophy. George B——, aged six, was admitted into Great Ormond Street Hospital on April 29, 1879, with general cardiac dropsy. He had had scarlatina with articular rheumatism six months before. After death the heart was found to be hypertrophied and still more dilated, weighing seven ounces—as large as that of a child of eleven or twelve. There was no valvular lesion of any kind, except dilatation of the orifice; and no history of any rheumatic affection previous to the scarlatina.

Look, again, at the case of Harold G——, with aortic regurgitation, previously mentioned. The first attack of rheumatism was only sixteen months before I saw him, and he had already enormous enlargement, chiefly dilatation, of the left ventricle. Observation of these cases in hospital shows that these changes advance at a rate unknown in later life.

As hypertrophy develops rapidly in children, so compensation is usually for a time exceptionally complete, and, as a further result of this effective compensation, great enlargement of the liver and spleen, pulmonary apoplexy, and extreme dropsy are rare in the younger children, becoming more common as age advances. It is an unusual thing to see a little child blue, turgid, and waterlogged—a sight so sadly frequent in the last stage of mitral disease in adults. Dr. Goodhart has observed these facts, and attributes them to reduction of the whole blood-supply as part of the general wasting, which is so conspicuous a feature. This probably plays some part in addition to efficient compensation. But there is still another reason. Children with severe heart-disease, as a rule, die from other causes before the stage of grave tricuspid leakage is reached. For in children the mode of death from mitral disease differs from that we see in later life. Instead of engorged liver and lungs, with blueness, extreme dyspnœa, and general dropsy, there is rapid wasting, progressive anæmia, feebleness, and death from asthenia rather than from the direct injury to the mechanism of circulation, unless it be the strangling grip of pericardial exudation and adhesion.

*Scarlatinal Rheumatism.*—The account of the various phases of rheumatism would be incomplete without some reference to the scarlatinal affection. An articular inflammation appears now and again in the course of scarlet fever, which can in no way be distinguished from that of acute rheumatism. It is often accompanied by endocarditis or pericarditis, and sometimes by chorea. Henoch[1] records

[1] *Diseases of Children*, p. 30 (Eng. Trans. Sampson Low, 1883).

a case in which acute arthritis appeared in the first week, followed by mitral murmur and chorea. This scarlatinal rheumatism, although it may come late, in most cases arises early; Dr. Barlow noted it as early as the third day.[1] In a series of cases observed by Dr. Ashby of Manchester the symptoms supervened with great regularity at the end of the first week. The endocarditis or pericarditis which comes late in the course of scarlatina are possibly uræmic; but uræmia does not set up inflammation of joints. Dr. Ashby inclines to the view that the arthritis is of septic origin, due to foul throat, or otitis, or empyema, and not a true rheumatism. The theory of septic poisoning, indeed, carries us a step further than the uræmic, for septicæmia produces arthritis as well as pericarditis and endocarditis; and septicæmia does undoubtedly arise in scarlatina in the way mentioned, as I have seen more than once. But then the articular affection of scarlatina is not especially associated with bad throats, or otitis, or empyema, or with other signs of septicæmia; moreover septicæmia will hardly explain early scarlatinal rheumatism, or the occasional concurrence of chorea. It seems clear that either genuine acute rheumatism does occur in the course of scarlatina, or else that

[1] *Brit. Med. Jour.* September 15, 1881, p. 510.

the scarlatinal virus itself occasionally produces an inflammation of joints and serous membranes, and a nervous choreic disturbance analogous to and indistinguishable from that set up by the rheumatic poison. It is curious to observe, too, as previously mentioned, that the especial liability to acute articular rheumatism, which is so marked in girls, extends to this scarlatinal form, as shown by Dr. Gresswell; the numbers being twenty girls to nine boys, the inequality between the sexes being most marked after ten years of age.

*Rheumatoid Arthritis.*—I had it in mind when I planned these lectures to say something of rheumatoid arthritis. But the shortness of time and the length of the subject prevent my finding place for it. I will merely say that, although it is uncommon in childhood, it does occur, and, as Sir A. Garrod long ago pointed out, sometimes in its most severe and intractable form. The disease in children appears to be due to the same causes as in later life, and to differ in no material respect from the type with which we are familiar in adults.

*Treatment.*—Almost the whole interest and importance of rheumatism in children centres in the cardiac inflammation and its results. The one great aim and object of treatment should be to minimise this danger as much as possible; and the first point which I would urge is the necessity of being constantly on guard against an insidious attack of endocarditis or pericarditis. I have shown how it may accompany the slightest articular affection—may even arise without accompanying arthritis of any kind; associated with chorea, or an exudative erythema, or an eruption of subcutaneous nodules; or it may arise apart from any known rheumatic phase with an indeterminate febrile attack of apparent insignificance. It is essential, then, to examine the heart carefully in every case of the slightest articular affection—even a stiff neck or a stiff knee; and in chorea, in tonsillitis, in erythema, in an evolution of nodules, and, indeed, in every pyrexial condition of every form. Whenever there is suspicion of rheumatic inflammation—even if no cardiac affection be perceptible—enforce absolute rest in bed. Complete physical repose and external warmth are of the first, possibly of vital, importance. Cases of slight rheumatism are, as a rule, treated far too lightly by both parents and doctors. What a vast difference it would have made in the future condition of the schoolboy, H. G——, for instance, if, instead of being allowed to follow athletic sports, and thus strain his heart's muscle and court fresh chill, he had been kept secure in rest and warmth. Dr. Sibson found that a much larger proportion of cases—more than two to one—treated by absolute rest escaped permanent heart-mischief than those allowed free action.

With regard to drugs, I may point out that the heroic treatment by large and repeated doses of salicylate of soda is rarely called for in the rheumatism of children, since the articular affection is usually slight, and the pyrexia as a rule not severe; for the salicylates appear to exert no favourable influence upon any rheumatic phase, except only arthritis and tonsillitis. Salicin may be given in place of salicylate of soda in most articular cases with advantage, as being less depressant—and with the salicin, alkalies. The general evidence of the statistics of the Collective Investigation Committee supports the conclusions of Dr. Fuller and Dr. Dickinson, that cardiac inflammation is less frequent and pronounced under their influence than under any other form of treatment. It would be interesting to note how full treatment by alkalies affects the development and duration of subcutaneous nodules, a point not yet ascertained.

## CONCLUSION

It remains only, Mr. President and gentlemen, for me to thank you cordially for the great honour you have done me in inviting me to deliver this course of lectures, and to thank my audience for their kind and indulgent attention to what I have laid before them.

# INDEX.

## ANÆ

ANÆMIA, in children, remarkable effect of rheumatism in producing, 41

Apoplexy, pulmonary, rare in young children, 115

Arthritis, symptoms of, 2, 3; only one manifestation of the rheumatic state, 3: most constant and prominent phenomenon of rheumatism in adults, 3; not representative in childhood, 4; may arise from various causes, 6; the rheumatic virus the most common cause, 6; its varying order in the rheumatic series, 10–22; proportion of the sexes affected at different periods of life, 23–26; the influence of family predisposition, 26–30; comparative insignificance of the articular affection in childhood, 30–34; rarity of hyperpyrexia in children, 34; examples of errors in diagnosis, 35–40; frequent association of tonsillitis with, 43; connection of chorea with, 51–66; scarlet fever specially associated with, 51, 52; harmony of incidence of arthritis, chorea, and choreic heart

## CHO

disease on the sexes from eleven to fifteen, 58, 99; rheumatoid arthritis, 118

CHOREA, 5; frequently set up by rheumatism, 6; disappears as maturity is reached, 8; its order of succession in the rheumatic series, 10–22; relation of, to rheumatism, 51–67; its slight affinity with other neuroses, 53; the influence of family predisposition, 53, 61–63; fallacy of the mimetic theory, 54, 55; minor form of, 55; effect of nervous shock and mental excitement, 55–57; data as to the degree of its rheumatic connection, 57–63; special proclivity of girls from eleven to fifteen to chorea, arthritis, and organic heart disease, 58, 99; the evidence of family history as to its rheumatic relation, 61–63; fallacy of ordinary statistics, 63–66; relation of nervous excitability to chorea and rheumatism, 67; its association with pericarditis, 82; and with endo-

## 124  INDEX

### DIL

carditis, 9.-100; the organic origin of the mitral murmur in, 96, 97

DILATATION, development of, 114

Dropsy; extreme rarity of, in young children. 115

Drugs, use of, in the treatment of rheumatism in children, 120

ENDOCARDITIS, commonly arises from rheumatism, 6; more frequent in children than in adults, 8; its order in the combinations of the rheumatic series, 10-22; characters of, in childhood, 92, 102; relation of, to rheumatism, 93, 100, 107; statistical evidence of the connection, 94, 98; its relation to chorea, 95-100; almost invariably found post-mortem in fatal cases of chorea, 96; the theory of strain or shock as the source of choreic endocarditis, 100; its relation to the evolution of nodules, 101-108; examples of the subacute progressive form, 102; similarity in morbid changes in valves and nodules, 103-108; microscopic appearance of mitral valve in a case of rheumatic endocarditis, 104, 106; rarity of the ulcerative form in children, 108

Erythema exudativum, frequently results from rheumatism, 6; its occurrence in the rheumatic series, 15, 19-21; statistical evidence

### HYP

of its connection with rheumatism, 46; various forms of, 47; appears mostly in the marginate and urticarious forms, 47; association of erythema nodosum with arthritis, 48; liability of young girls to erythema nodosum, 49

FAMILY predisposition, influence of, in rheumatism, 26-30; the evidence of statistics, 27; cases illustrative of, 28; children of rheumatic parents frequently anæmic, 41; its influence in chorea, 53, 61-63; rheumatic family history in 'growing pains,' 64

GIRLS, young, especially susceptible to arthritis, 24-26; to scarlatinal rheumatism, 25; to erythema nodosum, 49; to chorea and organic heart disease, 58, 59
'Growing pains,' rheumatic family history in, 64

HEART disease. in rheumatism, percentage of children and adults affected, 8; harmony of incidence on the sexes from eleven to fifteen of heart disease, chorea, and arthritis, 58, 99; significance of subcutaneous nodules in, 74-76. See Endocarditis, Pericarditis, and Mitral Stenosis

Hyperpyrexia, rheumatic, rarity of, in children, 33, 34

## HYP

Hypertrophy and dilatation, rapid development of, in children, 114; examples of, 115; the mode of death in children differs from that in adults, 116

MITRAL stenosis, proportion of the sexes affected, 109; arises most commonly in childhood, 109-111; evidence of its rheumatic relation, 110; earliest sign of, 111-114

NERVOUS excitability, its relation to rheumatism, 67

Nervous shock, as a factor in chorea, 55-57

Nodules, subcutaneous tendinous; 5; rheumatism the sole source of, 6, 7; at their maximum in early life, 8; their order in the rheumatic series, 10-22; importance of, as clinical signs of rheumatism, 69; common occurrence of, in children, 69; their character, distribution, and duration, 69-72; structure of, 72; their relation to rheumatism, 73; specially associated with the graver forms, 74; serious in proportion to their size and number, 74, 75; clinical significance of, 75, 108; their connection with grave forms of heart disease, 75, 76; examples of their association with pericarditis, 86-88; their pathological relation to fibrosis, 89; relation of, to endocarditis, 101-108; similarity of morbid changes in

## PUR

nodules and in valves in endocarditis, 103-108; microscopic appearance of a nodule in acute rheumatism, 105, 106

PERICARDITIS, 5; rheumatism the most common cause of, 6, 79; more frequent in children than in adults, 8; its varying position in the rheumatic series, 12-22, 79; the acute form rare in childhood, 80; examples of the acute form, 81-83; association of, with chorea, 82; characteristics of the disease in childhood, 83, 88; postmortem appearances, 84, 90; cases of the subacute form, 85-88; its association with nodules, 86-88, 101; significance of nodules in, 88; relation of nodules to fibrosis of the pericardium, 89; effect of thickened pericardium, 90; changes caused in the fibrous tissues of the pericardium by rheumatism, 107

Pleurisy, frequently an accompaniment of rheumatism, 5, 6; its position in the rheumatic series, 12-22; associated with rheumatism in two distinct ways, 76; two examples of primary rheumatic pleurisy, 77, 78

Polyarthritis, 3; synovialis, and rheumatica acuta, 3

Pulmonary apoplexy, rarity of, in young children, 115

Purpura rheumatica, 50; its probable connection with rheumatism, 50

126 INDEX

## RHE

RHEUMARTHRITIS, 3
Rheumatic, definition of the term, 2, 7
Rheumatic fever, the extreme expression of rheumatism in adults, 2
Rheumatic series of diseases, 6; arthritis, 6, 23–40; chorea, 6, 51–68; endocarditis, 6, 91–106; erythema, 6, 46–50; pericarditis, 6, 79–91; pleurisy, 6, 76–78; subcutaneous tendinous nodules, 6, 68–76; tonsillitis, 6, 42–46; varying order of the series, 10–12; clinical examples of combinations of, 12–22
Rheumatic sore throat, 43
Rheumatism, definition of the term, 2, 7; acute articular, symptoms of, 2; arthritis only one manifestation of the rheumatic state, 3; other morbid conditions prominent and constant in children, 4; of childhood most complete and representative, 4; developments of, 5; the rheumatic series, 6–22; broad conception of the disease, 7; in children, contrasted with that of adults, 7–10; varying order of succession of the rheumatic series, 10; combinations of the series, 12–22; the influence of sex, 23; statistics of the sexes at varying ages, 23; the influence of family predisposition, 26; statistics and examples of family predisposition, 27–30; the arthritis of childhood, 30–40; rarity of hyperpyrexia in children, 34; examples of mistaken

## SCA

diagnosis of arthritis in children, 35–40; the anæmia of, 41; connection of tonsillitis with, 43; characteristics of rheumatic tonsillitis, 43, 45; relation of erythema to, 46–50; purpura rheumatica, probably a minor expression of, 50; the connection of chorea with, 51–56; scarlet fever specially associated with arthritis, 51, 52, 116; relation of nervous excitability to, 67; frequency and importance of subcutaneous tendinous nodules in, 69; nodules specially connected with the graver forms of, 74; pleurisy occurs in connection with, in two distinct ways, 76; is the most common cause of pericarditis, 79, 107; association of pericarditis with other rheumatic phases, 79–88; relation of endocarditis to, 93, 97–100, 107; changes produced by, in the fibrous tissues, 107; the rheumatic origin of mitral stenosis, 110; scarlatinal rheumatism, 116; treatment of rheumatic children, 118; necessity of absolute rest and warmth, 119; the use of drugs in, 120
Rheumatoid arthritis, 118

SCARLATINAL rheumatism, susceptibility of young girls to, 25, 118; statistics as to the influence of sex in, 25; its connection with the phases of the rheumatic series, 116, 117
Scarlet fever, especially asso-

## SEX

ciated with acute rheumatism, 51, 52, 116
Sex, the influence of, in articular rheumatism, 23; proclivity of young girls to various phases of the rheumatic series, 24, 25, 49, 58, 109; harmony of incidence of arthritis, chorea, and organic heart disease on the sexes from eleven to fifteen, 58, 99
Sore throat, rheumatic, 43

## URT

TONSILLITIS, 5; frequently results from rheumatism, 6; its occurrence in the rheumatic series, 10-20, 43; its special connection with arthritis, 43, 44; characteristics of rheumatic tonsillitis, 44, 45

URTICARIA, associated with rheumatic disturbance, 47

www.ingramcontent.com/pod-product-compliance
Lightning Source LLC
Chambersburg PA
CBHW031338160426
**43196CB00007B/715**